BECOME A MESSAGE

Lajos Walder, Budapest, c. 1943

Lajos Walder

BECOME A MESSAGE

Poems

*Translated from the Hungarian
by Agnes Walder*

With a Foreword by Don Paterson

Upper West Side Philosophers, Inc.
New York

Upper West Side Philosophers, Inc. provides a publication venue for original philosophical thinking steeped in lived life, in line with our motto: philosophical living & lived philosophy.

Published by Upper West Side Philosophers, Inc. / P. O. Box 250645, New York, NY 10025, USA
www.westside-philosophers.com / www.yogaforthemind.us

Library of Congress Cataloging-in-Publication Data

Walder, Lajos, 1913-1945.
  [Poems. English]
  Become a message : poems / Lajos Walder ; translated from the Hungarian by Agnes Walder with a foreword by Don Paterson.
    pages cm
  Includes bibliographical references.
  ISBN 978-1-935830-30-6 (alk. paper)
  1. Walder, Lajos, 1913-1945--Translations into English. I. Walder, Agnes, translator. II. Title.
  PH3351.W35A2 2015
  894'.511132--dc23

                    2015002777

Typesetting & Design: UWSP
Printed in the USA

From your children to your children's children

CONTENTS

FOREWORD

Lajos Walder was born in Budapest in 1913, and died in 1945 in the Gunskirchen concentration camp, on the day it was liberated by the Allied forces. He had managed to graduate as a lawyer, despite the severe limitations on the number of Hungarian Jews allowed to pursue a university education. He was not, however, permitted to practice; instead he found work as a laborer in a factory. He continued to write and publish until the outbreak of the war, when he was recruited to a forced labor battalion. The details of Walder's impossibly tragic end I won't rehearse here; the reader is urged to turn to the afterword, where his daughter and translator Agnes Walder gives a moving account of his life.

Lajos Walder is unlikely to be a name you know or even half-know. And yet we should know it. Walder reads as a contemporary poet, in the best sense; though the reader will first be struck by Walder's refusal to play any of the familiar come-hither games of the modernist era (which have become so pervasive as to be invisible)—indeed before opening this book, they might first muster a sense of self strong enough to not be insulted by Walder's utter lack of need of them. Nonetheless despite his insistence that "poetry is a private matter," his voice is very far from indifferent, discourteous or cold. But it will speak the way it speaks, whether you are listening or not.

This vocal independence is most clearly signed by the fact that Walder does what the hell he likes, when he likes, and in whatever voice he likes. One minute he's shrinking the decades between author and reader to nothing, and in the next breath separating them by millennia. Who knows if Walder was aware of what was on the wind for him, but it seems to have dramatically sharpened and lengthened his perspective: every daily event seems to throw a historical, sometimes even a cosmological shadow. (His adventures in the space-time continuum are often very funny. "Interview" is a kind of science-fiction conversation with God; God had intended to get back to us and explain everything, or at least to the Neanderthal whose hand he was holding—but was momentarily distracted for a few million years.)

Stylistically, Walder had a deep bag of tricks. His favorite is to run logically with an illogical premise, and for much longer than he should be able to get away with; like Cocteau, he knew "how far to go too far." I can think of only a handful of other poets with the wit and nerve to pull that trick off—Francis Ponge, James Tate, and another writer he occasionally resembles, the great Scottish-Jewish surrealist comic Ivor Cutler. (In "Animal Tale" Walder reminds us that our reality is surreal enough; one merely needs to observe it clearly—in this case from the meat's perspective.) Though sometimes one feels a keen pang for the poet he would have been, had he lived: "Music for Prose" shows his ability to extend what another poet might have left as a local metaphor into an organizing conceit; in doing so, he reveals the soul of the modern metaphysical he could well have become. Those who die young do not have the luxury of juvenilia, but we should remember that these are a young man's poems. Some, like "Telephone"—where the poet is intoxicated by the potential of direct, immediate communication with anyone, anywhere—are a tad over-egged, and touching in their youthful over-enthusiasm. But all have their witty and ingenious merits, and many are plainly brilliant. "Horoscope," for example, sees the poet describe the statistical fates of nineteen children born that day (0.059 of them, for example, will be a movie star), and explain his plan to send their relatives one of his long-prepared death notices when the "quota" suicide or the car-crash victim eventually meets their fate. The poem is not only efficiently and hilariously executed but, in a smooth tonal gear-change oddly reminiscent of Billy Collins, manages to rise to a finely-judged lyric conclusion: "I, on the other hand, / will go dry-eyed to the window / and watch / how indifferently is washing his hands / in the autumn rain // an unknown, enormous Pilate."

Knowing the tragic details of his life, it's hard not to read Lajos Walder (or "Vándor"—"wanderer"—as he called himself in print) through the black lens of his biography, or—given the dreadful times in which he found himself living—as some kind of New Historical or cultural symptom. But he wouldn't have appreciated that, and was too much of a maverick to be usefully read in this way. Walder had no allegiance to any school or tradition. The bravery—more often it seems sheer recklessness—he speaks with are out of time. Of course he also speaks to his time, to his coevals, to the increasingly desperate economic and political conditions of pre-war Hungary; but his is also the thoughtless courage of a young Athenian calling out some venerable elder at a symposium, or some kid with a loudhailer at Occupy. His voice—brash, iconoclastic, dismissive of authority—is seized by the moment to the extent that it becomes the moment. Walder's presence is what survives here, and the experience of reading him is to return us sharply, wakefully, to our own present. It is the voice of an internal eternity, unconcerned with securing a future more than five minutes ahead. Walder is a nihilist; but he knows the value of nothing in a society which locates value in the wrong things entirely.

Where did these poems come from? Who or what is Walder like? Reading them for the first time, my mistake was attempting to place this poet at all. My knowledge of twentieth-century Hungarian poetry isn't sufficient to pin him to anything but the vaguest coordinates. I have no idea if Otto Orban encountered Walder's work in his youth; it's possible, and certainly it carries Orban's permanently raised eyebrow. Though I felt I could also hear the gallows humour of his Balkan neighbors, that cackling in the coal-cellar we find in everyone from Cioran to Charles Simic; then again, it also had the infinite world-weariness of Zbigniew Herbert, the flashy allegories of the young Miroslav Holub ... And lord knows Kafka is everywhere. His poetic sensibility, though, seems to me closest to the great Chilean anti-poet Nicanor Parra. Which is to say that like Parra, he is like no one at all. This is because poetry, as a subject, seems of little concern to him. Walder's interest was in what the poem could do.

While he may not have cared much about the effect he had on his readers, Walder was a natural communicator. Most poets are not. His genuine, gentle compassion is also a rarity in a poet. He also sees through everyone, through all our earthly and celestial masters: he won't deign to haggle with fascists or communists, argues strongly against the existence of Heaven, spoofs the very stars in the sky, and skewers the hypocrisies of humanism. (In "The Twenty-Five Letters of the Alphabet" he has the alphabet itself indict humanity: "We, who equally serve the British Empire / and the Hungarian Monarchy, / the Third French Republic and the Russian Soviet, / accuse the chief editor of the world's conscience / of successively committing / the gravest printing errors.") Walder's stance continually undermines the twentieth century's most cherished trope, that of 'identity'. He says simultaneously I am not one of you, and I am you—his point being that our identities are just as unstable as his. And he says this with great good humor, and in a delightfully capricious way with a metaphor: he is a star, he is a business, he is a hooker; he is a man stuck at a movie that bores him, he is a cloud, he is math; he is a thinking corpse, in a coffin on a train running between Paris and Bucharest. And he is also, openly, Lajos Vándor himself, the artist. Walder treats his own voice with as much respect as his others, but no more. He remains "always the other and always a stranger."

Agnes Walder's lucid and felicitous translation never reads like one of those 'labors of love' one has come to quietly dread, but the work of a direct descendant. She ends this fine collection as Walder surely would have done, with the line: "apart from thieves and murderers // there are also human beings." The human, the animal who is alone—yet cannot help but share the pain of its own kind. On every page, Walder reminds us that's who we are. That he was to suffer so barbarously at the hands of those who had forgotten is also his vindication: our humanity is poetry's only real subject.

Don Paterson

BECOME A MESSAGE

GATHER AROUND YOURSELF

Tour Guide as Foreword

Reader, you're now entering a museum
to observe a stranger (*Group Portrait of Myself*)
who has absolutely no idea about the meaning of his life
    (*Mr. Somogyi*).
He would like to scratch his head (*The Head*)
but not even that would help the future (*Horoscope*).
He realized that it was all in vain (*Short Lyrical Oration*),
even fairy tales prove a sad example (*Animal Tale*),
and the war is coming closer and closer (*Information*).
The seasons have passed over him (*Obligatory Spring Poem*),
and though he lives here (*Budapest*),
he is fleeing towards the stars (*Legend in Prose*).
He thinks of the plants as his siblings (*Family Event*),
and the animals, too, are of more interest to him (*Mooky*)
than HOMO SAPIENS (*Lost Generation*),
who is making ready to kill. (*Peace*)

Love rarely happens (*Expedition*),
though when he was an adolescent (*Manhood*)
he thought women were all different (*Parliamentarianism*),
but by now he only feels desire (*Reverence*)
and disappointment (*Commemorative Plaque*).

Lajos Vándor has lived twenty-four years to date (*Typewriter*),
yet has lived through humanity in its entirety (*World History*),
and even if he wasn't conceived in Original Sin (*Blood Pact*),
he, too, is just human (*The Human*)
and not a millionaire (*Poem of the Unemployed*).
He traveled the paths alone (*Arm in Arm*),
he was alone, and he will continue alone (*First Person Singular*)

because wherever he went (*Traveling*)
only the scenery changed (*Study Tour*):
he remained a picture frame (*Art Gallery*)
and a soul in uniform (*Budapest Division*).

I AM A WANDERER

—a modern monk
who wanders in a double-breasted suit.
All things I like just equally;
in the fields I dream about houses,
and in the city about evergreen pines.
I am a wanderer of millennia,
in Rome a Goth,
a German in Flanders,
I wore a toga and the Order of the Garter,
and wherever I was
I was always a stranger—
and at home, too—always just a stranger.
I am a wanderer—a frivolous modern poet,
an ode I write for as little as two pengős,
and let this quiet, simple offer of mine
not offend literary ears:
for ten pengős, a four-page short story
I will personally home-deliver.

I am a wanderer—a modern monk
who wanders in a double-breasted suit.
I was a trader in the temple of Jesus
and a publisher in Academia—
I was always the other and always a stranger,
always other than my own self:
in Rome a Goth,
a German in Flanders
on paper the writing,
in writing the letter,
in the fields I roofed houses,
onto the asphalt I sowed the seeds,
and even to myself I am a stranger:

because I was a German fighter in Flanders
and armistice in war—
I was always wholly other than myself,
the monk who wanders in a double-breasted suit.

In Rome I recited Greek poems,
kissed the hands of hetaerae—
I was always the other and always a stranger;
a petit-bourgeois in the nightclub
and in the soup kitchen a dandy.
I am a wanderer—a modern monk
who wanders in a double-breasted suit,
who would have liked to walk naked,
and knots his tie with care.
I was always the other and always a stranger,
always other than my own self:
in Rome a Goth, a German in Flanders
on paper the writing, in writing the letter—
in the fields I roofed houses,
onto the asphalt I sowed the seeds,
and even to myself I am a stranger.

I am a wanderer—a modern monk,
the lone wanderer of the eternal other.

RIDING ON CLOUDS

I am my moods' cuckolded Don Juan,
and half of Europe has fallen pregnant
from my daydreams.

Yesterday, the rising Sun
found me in flagrante with the Moon
and turned the horizon crimson
with embarrassment.

I didn't give it another thought,
and a couple of hundred steps on
approached a young cloudlet.

She was still a virgin,
and I hurriedly made her an offer—
lest someone else should beat me to it.

Then her face suddenly grew overcast,
fat teardrops fell from her eyes,
and when, half an hour after a domestic storm,
the sky cleared and
I hung my drenched heart
on top of the Eiffel Tower to dry,
I got to thinking
that once every streetwalker was a cloudlet.

This thought completely reassured me,
and I decided
not to run after Ladies in the sky anymore
because there are more than enough good-looking
    women on earth.

WE, THE TWENTY-FIVE LETTERS OF THE ALPHABET*

We, abcdefghijklmnopqrstuvxyz,
the twenty-five letters of the alphabet,
sadly draw our conclusions
about the current turn of events in Europe
and are willing, if need be,
to proclaim a general letter strike
even onto the forty thousand letters
of the Chinese alphabet—
if the European nations
do not alter
the top-secret foreign policy directives
handed to their ambassadors.
We, who equally serve the British Empire
and the Hungarian Monarchy,
the Third French Republic and the Russian Soviet,
accuse the chief editor of the world's conscience
of successively committing
the gravest printing errors.
We, who in Germanic or Latin shape were present
in every declaration of war and every peace treaty of
    the West,
accuse the historiographers,
who, by falsifying the history of humanity,
want to write bloody national chronicles.
We, who have been a Courths-Mahler romance
and the Zarathustra,
a Shakespeare comedy and a tragedy by Racine,

---

* Translator's note: the Hungarian alphabet consists of twenty-five
letters—a point further explained in the Afterword (p. 198).

protest against the new declarations of war,
whose plans can already be detected
in every nation's war ministry.
We, the twenty-five letters of the alphabet,
who, thanks to the good work
of lead miners and type casters,
are in the music books
of Swedish kindergarten children
and in Italian anatomy books,
who are in the Bible
and in the identity papers of war amputees,
protest against every enciphered telegram
and every political swindle,
which we know about but which others are not aware of
because:
we do not want to appear again
as names on the casualty lists
that the widows and orphans
will read through tear-filled eyes.
We, the twenty-five letters of the alphabet,
from 'A' through 'O' to 'Z',
demand world peace and demand equality before the law
and, having relinquished our autonomy,
are willing to shrink to a mere four letters
so that, in place of the pornograph and detective novels,
we may burn into human eyes one word:
'Love'.

FAMILY CHARACTERISTICS

You, my father, who gave the initial speed
to a perpetual motion
which one fine day
will turn into scrap metal within me,
and who from the atoms of your body
brought about
my first molecule
in spite of the fact that
you had not the slightest intention to do so—
I must confess—
this deed of yours is extremely dear to me!
It is no filial gratitude
which bows before you
under the influence of an archaic writing—
rather, the mind praises
the mindlessness
that brought about
your pleasure
and my life.
Because it takes courage
to seek our pleasure
if it's forbidden—
but if it's a permitted
pillage of the fruit,
then it stiffens one's spine,
since one submits to desire
with a thinking mind.
I bow before you,
you mustachioed
dead old man,
who heedlessly
fertilized

the worry in my mother,
and I believe
that through great new joys
I, too, will become
father and man!

INTERVIEW

Entirely free verse.

Strictly speaking, nobody is going to believe this—

in the afternoon, when Lajos Walder arrived home,
he was informed by his mother—
                    forty-seven years old
                    and her legs aching—
that someone was waiting for him
in the dining room.

The aforementioned, without a word, took off his coat—
                    they had bought it
                    four years ago
                    in Rákoczi street,
                    the shopkeeper
                    first said 156 pengő
                    but afterwards
                    let them have it for a hundred—
and went into the bathroom.

He washed his hands over the bathtub—
                    the landlord
                    had a new one installed
                    in the spring
                    because they had lived
                    in the house
                    for the past nineteen years
                    and were decent tenants—
dried his hands and entered the dining room.

"Good afternoon," he said in a polite voice,
"I am Lajos Walder."
A momentary silence followed—
                    "Il pleut, il pleut bergère,"
                    sang his brother
                    in the hallway—
then the stranger spoke:

"DELIGHTED," HE said briefly, "GOD."

Lajos Walder knew what war meant,
his father had been at the front
for four years—
                    as for one of his uncles,
                    he was caught by
                    a Romanian vanguard
                    and cut into eighteen pieces,
                    or perhaps it was
                    nineteen—
in other ways, too, he had a few experiences,
so he did not lose
his composure.

For a moment, he still hesitated
then the reporter woke in him—
                    he wrote fairy tales
                    for children's magazines
                    and contributed colorful reports
                    to weekly periodicals—
he reached into his drawer, took out some paper
and rummaged for a pencil.

"YOU WANT AN INTERVIEW," said a smiling GOD.
"AS A RULE HUMANS ASK BORING QUESTIONS.

I HOPE YOU WILL NOT BEGIN A SINGLE ONE WITH
'WHY', AND, ANYWAY, THERE ARE A FEW QUESTIONS
WHICH, FOR HIGHER REASONS, I WILL NOT BE ABLE
TO ANSWER."

"Sir," said Walder quietly,
"I am no longer an inexperienced reporter
who would harass you with such questions as
    why are we alive?
    what is the goal?
    from where?
    to where?
       etcetera ...
           because such things, for the most part,
           are of no real interest to the reader,
           and even if they were,
           bearing in mind censorship,
           the editor would cross them out anyway—
besides, I have far more
interesting questions,
for instance:

to what do we owe this honor?"

"A FEW SECONDS AGO," HE said, "I HAD SOME
MATTER TO ATTEND TO, AND I INADVERTENTLY LET
GO OF THE CAVEMAN'S HAND; AND SINCE THE
POOR CREATURE WAS HELPLESS BY HIMSELF, I WAS
CONCERNED THAT HE MAY HAVE PERISHED."

"I do not understand ... that a few seconds ... ago
... humanity's existence ... amounts only to that much ...
But, the age of Earth is accurately estimated at two billion

years, even according to the sages and the Hindu
philosophers it is that, roughly speaking."

"THIS IS ONLY A RELATIVE VIEWPOINT," replied GOD,
"EARTH—COMPARED TO THE LIFE OF MAN, IS
INDEED TWO BILLION YEARS OLD."

"I understand ... I fully understand," said Walder,
"... and how do you like him, Sir, the human,
and what he created?"

"PLEASE DO NOT WRITE THIS, BUT
CONFIDENTIALLY I CAN TELL YOU THAT IT IS AFTER
ALL PECULIAR WHAT THE NEWSPAPERS SCRIBBLE
ABOUT THE HUMAN MIND'S CREATIVE POWERS,
SINCE MAN HAS INVENTED NOTHING—HE MERELY
DISCOVERED WHAT HAS ETERNALLY EXISTED. NEW
THINGS—HE HAS NEVER CREATED, ALWAYS JUST A
PIANIST OF PHRASES, HE COPIES THE NOTES FROM
MY INFINITE SCALES, AND THAT'S HOW HE PLAYS."

"Sir," stuttered Walder with a heavy heart,
"what you are saying is tantamount to
b l a s p h e m y—a g a i n s t—h u m a n i t y,
according to this, everything is in vain,
and even Newton solved only one line
of the Giant Crossword Puzzle."

"YOU SPOKE CORRECTLY," came the gentle reply,
"ALL THE TRIUMPHS OF THE HUMAN MIND
CONSTITUTE BUT A FEW LINES OF ETERNITY'S
INFINITE MONOLOGUE."

"Sir," said Lajos Walder, hopeful—
                    the first mariner had long ago
                    circumnavigated the Cape of Good Hope
                    and proudly reflected on
                    how powerful man is—
"could you not leave me with a heavenly sign
so that people would believe me when I tell them:
you were here and commented thus?"

But by then there was no one else in the room,
                    and for dinner
                    he ate
                    scrambled eggs,
Lajos Walder,
chief editor of humanity.

GOD, on the other hand,
hurried directly
to a Conference on Star Issues
to listen to the complaint of Uranus,
whose territorial integrity was being threatened

                    —by a stray comet.

ARM IN ARM

Nowadays
I walk arm in arm
with myself.

People
look curiously
at this mysterious couple

and do not know

whether
the woman is kept
or
the man is a gigolo?

I exchange glances
with those women
who have

masculine eyes

my partner
looks at those men

who can gaze femininely.

And this is how we stroll
among the bankrupt shops
and the purchasing opportunities
of the boulevard—

and what we dream about
is
that once
every human

was two humans:

a woman
and a man.

REVERENCE

I mourn every woman
who lives and is not mine

because for me they are dead.

I tie a long black veil
onto my desires
and immediately notify
my sense organs
about the calamity.

As a punishment:

I will not dream about them anymore,
and since I caught them in the act
with someone else

I immediately commence
divorce proceedings

against—my imagination.

SHORT LYRICAL ORATION

I am the last ambassador
and the last depot
of ideology-free
European literature.

My castles in the air
are no longer airtight,
and starlets
blur before me
the real stars.

In vain I toll
my feelings' manufactured
death bell—

that Europe is a sinking ship
and I do not want to drown
in salt water—
that the sons of Gandhi in India
are steaming the salt
to national colours

and before long
the sea will be saltless.

I am therefore not angry
with anyone
because if I were angry
it wouldn't matter,

since today everybody
is his own publicity chief,
printing error
and female cousin—

love itself falls under luxury tax,

and among the many places of worship,
little by little,

they lose God.

TELEPHONE

Any second now I can make contact
through the electric circuitry
of European Nations.
All I have to do is ask the telephonist,
and I can even call South America
from here—my room.
I can find out the exact time
and which exhibitions are on

because today they installed a telephone
in our home.

The appliance is untouched,
I haven't yet called anyone and no one has called me,
and I'm still pondering
who should be first on my list.

I could call aunt Gizelle,
it's her birthday tomorrow,
and there's no way I'll be able to congratulate her in
        person;
or, I could call up my tailor
to find out when he'll be sending my overcoat,
promised for yesterday.

I could, but I won't.
The appliance is still silent.
There is no current going through it,
and I feel that the first call
should be to someone more significant than these ...

because, look—you might not understand it—
for me this black machine right now
represents civilization.
I've got it. I'll call up Mussolini, or Eden,
and explain to them:

Look, Gentlemen, you are both family men,
unlike Hitler.
So, let's talk intimately for once
as fathers, husbands and sons do—
especially because it's about
fathers, husbands and sons.

I'm well aware there is a ton of goodwill
in you both, it's just that the rules
of international diplomacy are somewhat rigid,

so make yourselves comfortable.

Mr. Eden, why don't you take off your hard collar,
and you, Signor Mussolini, loosen that gun belt
around your belly just a notch.
(*Apologies, perhaps that word isn't appropriate,*
because for someone so high above the rest of us
you might not even have a belly).

Gentlemen, let us at last have a good chat,
though you don't even know who I am!

I'll tell you:

I am the representative
of approximately 150,000,000 young European men

who, in the absence of physical impairment,
are fit for military service.

Now do you understand me?!
Because, please, believe me,
it amounts only to this:
that we talk to each other as human beings,
Mr. Eden, Signor Mussolini—
then it will most certainly not come to pass
that one of us shoots first—at the other's child,
since that would make him a common murderer!

See, we've already made progress
because a well-meaning person
can always make himself understood by the other.
Animosity—irreconcilable, bloody animosity—
only occurs between two soldiers
pointing bayonets at each other,

but only until they are wounded—
then they're human beings once more.

That's what I would say
to Mussolini or Eden
if I, the petit-bourgeois,
could also have a say in the fate
they are planning for me.
But, unfortunately, it cannot be.

The telephone is still untouched,
and since I want to act in the spirit of our times:

I should make the first call to the lunatic asylum.

THE HEAD

His boss, in a fit of rage,
called him in and abused him—

what was the meaning of this:

Yesterday, twice he had left off
the dot from the letter 'i',
and anyway—
his bookkeeping was very careless.

He stood in the doorway
with tears in his eyes,
and it flashed through his mind
that now they'll throw him out
      "tomorrow I'll be unemployed again," he thought,
      "what will my poor mother say."

To the Boss he would have liked to reply:
      "I work unceasingly
      in place of two,"
but he just stuttered,
no voice escaped his throat,
and in his confusion,
as the saying goes,

he completely lost—his head.

Naturally, they looked for it everywhere,
poked with the broom
even under the cupboard,
but his head, which he firmly stated
he had brought with him

to the office that morning,
was never found again.

Later, he reported it to the police
and advertised in every daily
that in such and such a place
at such and such a time

he had lost his head—size 56.

The others were astounded to read the news
and shook their necks,
that not so long ago,
there still lived among them
a person

who, in accordance
with the ancient, outdated custom,
wore a head

under his hat.

HOROSCOPE

I stick a black flag on my forehead,

and with self-esteem lowered to half mast,
I decree the official mourning:

because in our town today
nineteen people were born.

Statistics lie before me

> and just like the star gazers
> searched for destiny
> among the heavenly signs
> when a royal child
> was born

I pore over them
trying to find the answer to:

what will be their fate.

2 will die young of lung disease,
1 will die a hero, 0.059, however, will be a movie star,
3 tax-paying citizens, 1 a notorious criminal,
2 unemployed, and again 1—a streetwalker;
4 of the women among them will on average have 2
children (on average, because 3 will have no children,
while the 4th will bring 8 into the world);
1 will commit suicide, 2 will have venereal disease,
and 1 will become the victim of a fatal traffic accident.

This will be the fate of 18, whilst the 19th
can only be expressed
in the 10,000ths:
that one will become the President of a Republic,
a banker, the world champion in 100-meter sprint,
or remain a virgin into extreme old age.

I know—now I should be lying
like a fortune teller on a home visit, who,
inspite of ominous signs,
prophesies a phenomenal path for the newborn.

I rather not say anything,

instead, all day long, I write telegrams of condolence
and whistle Chopin's funeral march.

And when the day arrives:

that they commit suicide
or get run over by a tram,

I take out the completed death notice
from the appropriate card index,
address it

and dispatch it to the relatives.

Then they will assuredly cry
because it will occur to them
that one day they, too,
will have to die—

I, on the other hand,
will go dry-eyed to the window
and watch

how indifferently is washing his hands
in the autumn rain

an unknown, enormous Pilate.

ANIMAL TALE

"Sir," said the veal goulash
in a pained voice
and started to weep.

"Appealing
to your most sacred family sentiments,
I implore you—please,
listen to my sad story.

My father was the village bull—

you can imagine
how much my poor mother
cried on account of it,
and their married life
was not at all exemplary.

In vain
did my father try to explain
that he did this for a living,

my mother did not believe him—

and we all knew
what it meant
when he said,

'For business reasons,
I have to go.'

It almost broke my mother's heart!
You, Sir, doubtless have heard
one or two things

about the maternal heart—

My mother's heart
is currently liverwurst
in a first-rate butcher shop
on the boulevard.

My little sister
was sacrificed to capitalism.
Our farmer syphoned away
her mother's milk,
and without it
she couldn't overcome tuberculosis ... she died.

My nephew is Transylvanian goulash
in a Globus conserve,
and my grandfather,
the government-pensioned village bull,
is currently salted meat

in a Norwegian cold room.

Oh, Sir, forgive me
for disclosing to you
my sad family connections.

Please, offer
your condolences

and say an expiatory prayer for us

whenever you read
in the obituary
that a kilo of veal chops
costs one-fifty."

INFORMATION

It was dark and I was at
the outskirts of town
when the Angel approached me.
        Murrillo's angels were
        not like this one—
        nor is the guardian angel
        who, in the oleograph,
        watches over
        the little orphan girl
        as she traverses the plank
        across a fast-flowing stream.
"I am the Angel of Death," said this
stout, well-bred man of average height;
and, producing his personal credentials
inclusive of photograph,
he obligingly identified himself.
It really was him.

"Behold—the end," I mumbled sadly,
and I thought of my mother.
        They say that
        for the dying,
        in his last moments,
        the greatest events
        of his life
        crowd into recall—
I thought of my mother,
and of Petőfi, who died
in battle,
and of Heine,
who died in his mattress-grave,
because, as I looked around me,

I saw that I was standing in front
of a dry-cleaning establishment.
"Mr. Angel," I said in an acrid voice,
"for me, this is excessive poetic symbolism
at the moment of death,
for soon I will arrive in Hell,
where, in the fires of purgatory,
I will be cleansed like a used
deerskin glove."

"Oh," said the embarrassed Angel of Death,
and pushed his slightly greasy hat
high onto the crown of his bald head.
"On this occasion
I have no wish to talk to you
about your personal affairs.
On the contrary,
I want, so to speak,
to ask you for a favor:

I am in need of a little information."

"Information? From me? Regarding what?"
I asked surprised. "And ..."
But the Angel of Death would not
let me finish the sentence.

"I want to learn a thing or two about humanity,"

said he in a confidential tone.
"Naturally, we do not expect your services
free of charge ...
back scratches back," he added with a cunning look
and fell expectantly silent.

"I don't fully understand," I replied honestly
and saw that the Angel of Death
considered me decidedly stupid.
Nevertheless, he made an effort to be polite
and started to explain.

"Please bear in mind," he said,
"that we are in constant business contact
with humanity.
In peacetime, this means steady, quiet business,
just enough for a bourgeois existence,
because, pray, we are a big family
up there.

But now they say
there will be war.
I must admit, we have made a few
excellent transactions with Xerxes,
during the Crusades, with Napoleon,
and then in the World War.

But in the last few years
there have been so many suicides, Sir,
that slowly
we, too, are beginning to be convinced

that life doesn't have much purpose!

So, I'm sure you can understand
that it makes no sense
for us to tire ourselves
with the creation of a new war,
if people are already
killing themselves in large numbers
or are dying of TB, etcetera.

I think our policy is straightforward:
we will only make the deal
if we can secure
first-class references
about humanity."

"Sir," I answered furiously,
unable to hide my indignation,
"you came to the right person!
A shoddier, more dull-witted gang
you could not find, even among the jackals.
Every effort is futile:
they have never been good,
and they are not improving."

The Angel of Death looked at me in surprise;
at first he thought
that I craftily wanted to divert
his attention from business.
But then, when he saw
that my outburst was honest
he didn't even answer.
My disclosure visibly depressed him.
Then, after a brief reflection,
he took his collapsible wings
out of his inside pocket,
lit a cigar and flew away.

And since then, whenever I read in the papers that
"the Great Powers are approaching each other with
        understanding,"
that "the new session of the League of Nations
strengthens European peace," or that
"Germany sits down to negotiate
with France,"

a cold shiver runs down my spine,
and the thought flashes through my mind
that in some out-of-the-way corner,
like a nervous stock broker
with a sure tip in his hand,
crouches the Angel of Death,
excitedly waiting
for humanity to improve just that little bit,
and for relationships to improve

because then—
he will instantly strike that business deal

which means
new War and old Death.

BUDAPEST

The foreign language travel brochures describe her
as "The Queen of the Danube"—
that, perhaps, is a little too excessive.

Rather, she resembles
the proprietress
of a love institute.

At first she started out as two women: Pest and Buda,
but when it occurred to her
that she would then always need two new hats
and two new pairs of stockings,

her business sense prevailed,
and she became one woman.

Her marital status is shrouded in uncomfortable mystery
because in spite of the fact that she is a maiden,
thus far, she has already given birth
to fourteen healthy suburbs,

and what, from the point of view of tourism,
is most embarrassing—

each one of them bears the name of a different father.

Her well-wishers say of her that she is a widow
who supports herself and her children
by renting out rooms—

poor widow: she has about 1,000,000 lodgers,
and aside from official superintendence
she is also involved
in other business dealings.

If the truth be known: she is a barmaid
who appeals to foreigners in the artificial light of night,
but whoever has seen her towards dawn
in her asphalt-coloured bed-jacket
will never again feel any inclination towards her.

By the way, she is not ashamed to work, and
if, around the end of the month, she is occasionally
    squeezed,
she stands out above the Danube and with a voice
hoarse from smoking and being up all night:

"come in beautiful boy," she calls
to the Great Plain.

LEGEND IN PROSE

Six days ago,
God put in an order

for the earth and the sky.

The universe, rushing feverishly,
finished the urgent work,
and by Saturday morning delivered it.

God
put the whole thing on his table,
and from the shining, colored wrapping paper
unwrapped—reality.
As for the wrapping paper—he promptly threw it away.

A few seconds later
an angel arrived, out of breath.

>   "My Lord, you lost something," he said,
>   and produced the colored wrapping paper.

The Lord looked at him, surprised.

>   "Come now," He said,

and with His invisible finger
pointed to Earth,

>   "surely this is reality, this is the essence—
>   what you hold in your hand is—nothing—
>   merely sparkle, colorful decoration, appearance!"

The angel despaired quietly.
Then the rebellious words
broke through his silence.

> "Could it be possible that the sparkle is—nothing—
> and that the grey reality is the essence?
> But then life isn't worthwhile!"

God gave this some thought.

> "Alright," He said gently,
> "for you, let reality be: nothing,
> and let the sparkle be: the essence."

The angel was about to leave.

> "What is it they call you, son?" asked the Lord.

Bowing gratefully,
the angel introduced himself:

> "I am the poet," he said. Then he left.

The Lord gazed after him thoughtfully.

> "Poor thing," He thought, "assuredly, he will starve to
> death."

This thought troubled Him,
so He summoned all the stars
and prevailed upon them
to watch over—the poets.

The stars heeded the Lord's command,
and it is since that time
that there is such an extraordinarily good relationship
between—the stars and the poets.

That is to say, when the poets
look up at the stars—

they instantly forget about being hungry.

LAST HUMAN BEING

To the Editor,

Sir, I'm writing to you,
I, the last human being on earth,
because aside from me there is no one—
only generals and managing directors.
Everyone here is either a socialist
or belongs to the Hitler party and wears a brown shirt,
though there are one or two
other interesting types:
the unemployed and the real-estate magnate.

The saddest thing is
that there isn't a woman next to me.
There are of course females on the street corners
who sell for cash
the possibilities of five-minute carnals,
but a woman capable of being virtuous
for a long time
now is only to be found in the museum.

Although there are many around me,
not one of them can understand my words,
and if I say that I am hungry—
munching, they laugh in my face.

Yet I live,
and in the street fusillade
I bandage everyone's wounds
as well as my own,
which I receive equally from all directions.

And I contemplate,
I, the last human being,
and I weep for the Greek sages
that they were sages and not animals,
because everything—everything here has been in vain,
the result would never have been different.

I contemplate,
I, the last human being,
who will die tomorrow,
who, even when he ate salted fish with onions,
nurtured beautiful dreams.

Sir, please, forgive me
for delivering my own eulogy,
but the priests do it for money,
and I've never had any money.

Sir, I will die tomorrow,
and with me culture will die.
And the day after tomorrow,
there will not be a human being on earth,
only a Nazi and a communist.

AUTOBIOGRAPHY

When my father,
without our prior consent,
died unexpectedly, leaving us behind
on the first of May without rent,
I believed that the Mightiest was the landlord.
But when the tax collector
took away the bed
from under my sick mother,
I realized
that the State watches over its citizens.
From then on
I did not wear my hat whacked on to one side
because the thought kept tormenting me—
what would then be left for the other side?
Every morning I salted my tears,
and dried up the dewy meadows,
till once, on a fine day,
one of my tightrope-walking friends,
having lost his emotional equilibrium,
died of blood poisoning.
The next day, I read
in a daily
that the global economy
finally found its lost equilibrium,
and I mourned for my friend
that he could not wait one more day.
I sank my eyes into infinity,
whereupon my doctor
diagnosed a pit in my stomach.
It was then that
I had my brand-new identity turned inside-out,
and, getting my coat button sewn onto my skin,

I decided
to give up all logical mental activity.

That is just what happened. And soon after,
I became a university professor.

MOOKY

If you really want to know, we found him:
my sister brought him home one autumn evening.

He came into the room
with the look of one
who doffs his hat for no one—
and, if he were able,
would doubtless hang his two thumbs
into the slits of his waistcoat.

"Hello, boy," he said with his eyes
when he caught sight of me.
   "I am an American citizen,
   a free nation's—free citizen—
   I hope you understand,"
   he added with a grin,
   "what the difference is between us,"
   and gave a supercilious bark.

Later he also made it known to me
that he did not rate preconceptions highly,
and when I asked him
his opinion about house training,
   he energetically declared
   that such was the privilege
   of pedigreed little dogs
   whereas he was strictly a democrat.

We never inquired about his heredity.
An acquaintance of ours musingly remarked
in connection with him—

how inscrutable
must be
the ways of Dog Providence—

that a genealogist who undertook
to shed light upon his ancestry,

in place of a family tree,
would find a crossword puzzle—
wherein horizontally and vertically
all the dog breeds of the world
would appear.

He was not at all choosy,
from garlic to grapes
he ate everything,
and if I'd smoked better-quality cigarettes,

after lunch he would surely have lit one.

The newspaper and the radio were of no interest to him,
he was a confirmed pacifist;
and as a babe of the postwar generation,

he held that even the cat—was just a dog.

Then one day, when he realized
that he had to stand on two legs for a mouthful

in the dead of winter—just as he came, he quietly
      vanished;

I put on black clothes in his honor,
and as a mark of mourning

(it was his favorite food)
ate 10 decagrams of kolbász for dinner.

And now, like a new-age Virgil, I write the new type of
   epos:

I sing of dog and bone and versify about a stray little
   mongrel,
who wanted and managed to be free—in a slave age.

TEN COMMANDMENTS

In a town whose population is sixty percent bronchitic,
it's not on account of Ministerial Regulations
that you should not drive with a faulty exhaust—
just because
you don't kill, steal, commit adultery or
don't turn away the needy from your door,
you won't be more meritorious than others
since you are acting under the influence
of thousands of years of hallucination.
But when your conscience,
having risen above sly tax evasions,
commands you to stop
for a little chick ambling across the road,
then you have arrived at your Lord,
and you may celebrate the Human Being
in yourself.
Until then, you will erect enormous edifices in vain,
where you demonstratively praise God
with the profit
which He took for you from your fellow men.
You burn large candles in vain,
hysterically calling atheist
the one who prays inwardly.
Whatever you do for fear of regulations
is not greatness,
and it isn't true
that God forgives repentant sinners,
because even if you forgive yourself
you can't be sure that you'll be forgiven
by the one you sinned against.
So don't just be concerned
whether the light is red or green,

rather remember
that we will all die one day,
and don't imagine
that your good deeds will weigh more in the balance
if, while speeding at a hundred,
you run your two-ton limo
over a lame beggar and
then, having had mass said for the salvation of his soul,
you give a quarter of a million in compensation
to the smiling heirs.

ESSENTIALLY A REVISED EDITION

Love thy neighbour as he loves you,
because hating someone
who harms you
is just as great a virtue
as loving someone who is of no use to you.
Because it's not morality that is greatness,
rather greatness itself is morality—
just try cheering Mussolini
in Moscow,
they'll teach you with a whip
that greatness creates its own moralities.
Precisely for this reason,
whoever throws a stone at you,
don't throw bread back at them,
because the price of bread
is already forty-four cents a kilo.
Be glad therefore, if in our chronic unemployment
you have enough
for your daily needs.
Since the proverb that says,
"The dog barks, the caravan moves on,"
is mistaken—
because there comes a time when all dogs get hoarse,
and at such times
the members of the caravan start barking—
therefore, do not squander away
your pawn tickets,
but collect them right up to the hour of your death,
and don't forget the commandment:
Do not commit adultery;
in today's tough economic situation

just be grateful
that you can support
your own legitimate
children.

JAZZ ANTHEM

... how the Tango beats,
the rhythm rocks
and the banjo twangs
... how the blood quickens,
the bodies swoon
and the trombone whines.
In piercing,
blunt dimness
of blue-red lamps
blooms the burning union
of marriageless bodies.
Oh, Jazz! Our souls'
half-realized
wild rush
from the depth of worry
to the distant fields
of bewitching desire ...
Oh, Jazz! I adore you,
because you stoke my blood
with willingness!
Saxophone, trombone
cornet, violin
and screaming piston,
restless souls
forged together
from wood and metal.

No one will understand
centuries from now
why the primitive noise
of a tapping little drum
wooed me.

I believe in you—my strange
rhythmically-quivering
wild music,
because that's how
the blood pulses in my veins
and, akin to you,
makes music.
I believe in you,
trembling of human bodies
gathered in a musical instrument!
The sobbing of desire
screeches in my veins,
with lusting great rhythm
expecting the whole:

of Life.

CIRCLE

... and he kept on going, going, going, going—and he could not break free from the circle. Yet he felt that the circle would strangle him because he came from it and returned to it.

What he wanted was to leap forward—constantly waiting for the circle to split open and be flung out into infinity along his own parabola.

He wanted to leap forward—because he felt that the circle would strangle him! At first, he tried to rebel, but they put terrible shackles on his legs, and he realized that there was no escape.

He realized that the circle was everything—and that outside the circle there's nothing else but the gallows, and inside the circle there's nothing but bourgeois death.

But he was young and he wanted to live!

... and he kept on going, going, going because at least then he was fed, and if he stopped lashes of the whip would rain upon his back—and the fitful snarls of those who came after him. He didn't sing, he didn't laugh, he just kept on going, going, going, going because by then he knew that one had to keep on going.

And when the cherry trees had burst into flower for the twentieth time and his blood had long been boiling, one night, as much as his shackles allowed, he distanced himself from the circle and timelessnessed into love. And after that again and again, and more greedily—because he felt that this was the only way to escape from the circle.

Then the enamel chipped off his teeth, and he didn't mind trudging in a circle anymore—because it was well-trodden and the road ahead straight forward; and he kept on going ... going ... going ... going ... then the circle came to an end, and he perished into nothing ...

TRAVELING

My body is only third class,
and in it, incognito, travels—the soul.

Who knows? Perhaps in another world it is king
or a secret envoy
whom God is sending on a particular mission:

from my birth—to my death.

My body rushes on invisible tracks,
scenery glides before my eyes,
new faces appear,
old ones vanish in my memory,

and gradually the traveling begins
to tire me.
Occasionally, I alight,
I look at my mother or at a girl—

and then on a shaky wooden bench
with a single flower—the sum total of my luggage—
the soul travels on with me.

My body is only third class,
in it, incognito, travels the soul—

and I know that one day
out of my grasp will
hesitantly spin
my serialized travelogue:

life.

DUST CLOTH

As cheekily as

    a dust cloth

which, contrary to official regulations,
is shaken
out the front window—

I hang in space.

Someone's holding me by the collar,
and I wriggle around a fair bit

but not too much

because if I were let go
from that grasp
I would crash like a shooting star
and at some spot

I know
I would hurt myself badly.

So I stay put,
inhale the splendid air

and, if I see a star that
has not been bathed,
or a schoolchild
is very sleepy in the morning—
well, I go over

and wipe their eyes.

Truth be known, I'm just a rag
which, when wiped over things,
will instantly make them shine brightly—

so what do you think,

couldn't humanity do
with a bit of spring cleaning?

GROUP PORTRAIT OF MYSELF

For a long time now
I haven't made a dynastic issue of myself,
and not by any means am I multiplying:

Neither First, nor Second,
Nor Sixteenth,

I am simply
just Louis.

Strictly speaking just ex-Louis,

an economy stove's blazing flame,
half-hearted hero,
retired revolutionary.

Once in a while, though, we still meet
the elementary-school Louis and the others,
the dreamer, the cynic, and the secondary-schooler,
the good boy, and the one others disapprove of.

We talk to each other honestly
about what cannot be redeemed:

Just how was it?
And what could have become
of at least one of the Louis
amongst us.

And at the end of the family counsel
uncle photographer pops up,

and the many Louis
gather around me with serious faces:

    I sit in the middle,
    and at my feet, as is proper,
    lies the kindergartner.

Then they go away.

And the one who remains
is neither the First nor the Sixteenth

just the identity papers

of someone
who is not identical.

ODE TO A FREE VERSE

Time and again I'm so embarrassed because of you—
you just don't have any ambiance.
Other poets write such beautiful poems,
but you are so ugly, my child.

Wicked images spurt from your lines,
sarcastic words, tendencies here and there.
And you yourself are as ill-behaved
as one, who without a mother, was given birth
by your father.

Look! Every poem of another poet
behaves correctly in society,
entertaining the grandmother
and the innocent demoiselle of the house alike.

But you, my boy, lead a bachelor's life,
it's just lucky that you are of neuter gender.
If you were a girl, you'd surely be unchaste
and give birth to illegitimate verse.

Oh, this is not a reprimand, since you may even
raise a hand at me with total indifference
to your pitiful longevity on earth,
unlike others' well-brought-up poems.

But I understand you, since you've never had a proper
     upbringing,
because you were born grown-up, my child,
and while other poems tooted on little pipes
instead of playing on rhymes—with you—life played.

And I don't care what they say about you!
If they hurt you, I'll always stand behind you
because I was compelled to abort you—

nine months felt too long for my doubts.

A POET LIVES HERE AMONGST YOU

"A poet lives here amongst you," I keep telling myself,
each time I climb the stairs to the second floor,

but the underjanitor doesn't even look at me,
and the rude little maid
throws the garbage directly onto my head
from the third floor,
the janitor, on the other hand, pretends
that he hasn't noticed I'm going his way
and accidentally, in a loud voice, explains
to our neighbour

that I already owe him five late-entry fees.

I am decidedly ashamed of myself—
two of my books have already been published,
very good reviews were written about me,
I appear on radio as well—
but it seems that poetry
is still not a respectable-enough occupation
in this neighbourhood.

Of course, the underjanitor always
greets the window cleaner in advance,
not to mention the corner grocer,
who likewise lives in our building
(owing to which fact, sooner or later, our building
will be proclaimed a historic monument)

"A poet dwells here amongst you," I mumble on,
despairingly,

so as to gain some prestige
at least before myself—
unfortunately it doesn't work:

our building is in Joseph Town,

where instead of poems
people read their savings books,
and nowadays, not even on Sunday,

will they put on airs.

TOPIC FOR AN EDITORIAL

You, who write about misery and suffering
as your salary is raised to two thousand,
and, having had the soul of Christ made into a tuxedo,
wear in your buttonhole
Compassion's Legion of Honor—

You, an Apostle with a Savings Account,
who shed tears over the starving,
and, since nowadays it is the cheapest,
pray to God for them—

Whose words are empty rockets
which leave a person hungrier,
and whose intention is just flashy advertising
and an opportunity for a new volume of poetry—

You, who are a role model for the middle class
and will go to Heaven by car—

      Mr. Editor,
I'll only say this much:

It makes no difference if a person in the desert
dies of thirst ten steps from a well,
or runs around jobless in Budapest
and dies of hunger in front of a grocery store.

COMMEMORATIVE PLAQUE

I've never yet had
a two-room, all-amenities woman
in my life.

Someone else was always
the husband or the lover,
and I

always just the subtenant.

It's true, though, that
I had no rent worries,
and as others paid
for central heating,

it was warming me—

but while other men
with prudent foresight
banked their amorous savings
into the current account
of perpetuating the human race,

I felt that I've been
a statutory official
elected to overcome
women's sexual misery.

For this very reason,
I would like to place upon every woman
who had ever been mine

a commemorative plaque—

because I think that
it would make far more sense
if, rather than on the façades of houses,

it were on the bodies of women

that the poet's place of residence
and duration of stay

were commemorated.

STUDY TOUR

Each day a person meets
with something new
which he thinks

    no one has ever
    lived through before him

and then a novel
gets in his hands
or someone complains

    and in an instant
    it dawns on him

that what was new to him
is identical for everyone.

    At such times—

he feels as if he were
on a study tour
in which every person
takes part once

    and wherever they go
    the Great Tour Guide explains

sometimes pointing to the right
sometimes to the left

this—is love
that—is relinquishment
and that, over there—

is whooping cough.

THE HUMAN

I am a human,
or, if you prefer,

the deficit
showing on the closing statement
of the universe.

I have twelve pairs of ribs.
This is of no great concern to me,
but half of the thirteenth
is missing—
and that does get me thinking.

Well, what is a human?

My siblings: the proletaires,
and my half siblings: the capitalists—

a crowded bedsitter
of suffering
which they have forgotten
to wallpaper to perfection—

And ever since,
like flawed merchandise,
from the harmony of nature
he was rejected:

on the first of every month
he gives notice to the landlord

and on every fifteenth
he stays on.

REPORT

Miss Mabel Faithful is my name,
I'm a famous reporter.
I've already flown over the Himalayas
and had rapport with the stars in the sky.

I've done a report on Hitler,
the Duce gave me an interview;
this morning my chief editor asked me
to write on "what is love?"

First up, I asked a streetwalker:
"Love," said she, "could be
if the punter pays for an hour,
and it's over in ten minutes."

Then I inquired of a lady
who sat in her bath,
a trifle plunged in thought,
she put a blasé smile on her face:

"Love is: four rooms, central heating, all comforts,
silver fox, the opera and bridge parties—
and whatever else love is,
forget my husband,
ask Charlie."

Next in turn was a teenage girl,
the poor thing looked at me tearfully:
"Love is if, perchance,
during philosophy class
the teacher touches my hand."

After this, I made a pilgrimage to Verona
to visit Juliet's grave—
and she instantly started complaining
that it's become hopeless with Romeo.

"His fire and kisses are not as of old,
he no longer embraces me the way he did
four hundred years ago,
not as ardently, not as besottedly
gone is the raptured frenzy."

"But Juliet," I said, "by now you're only dust!"
"Am I only dust?" she asked coldly.
"Then let Romeo turn into a vacuum cleaner,

and you can write

that is love."

FIRST PERSON SINGULAR

As if at a boxing match
I watch myself from the ringside,
how the individual in me struggles

with the collective ideas.

The first round
was a tie:

I was young, and I thought
that the many
is more than the one,
but in the crowd
the truth got lost,
and now I say
enough is enough!

I renounce that stupid herd,
which entrusts itself to the instincts of others—

because I have never seen
two thousand human beings together,
because if there were two thousand of them somewhere:

they were no longer humans.

"Crucify him"—that's what they always shout,
and they always crucify the best
or lament at the base of the cross

that they missed out on seeing this rare spectacle.

I—from now on and forever,
see every human being in the first person singular,
because whoever suffers
and is wretched on earth

is always lonely and always alone.

I—from now on and forever
see every human being in the first person singular,

and I am not the brother of a hundred thousand,
only of one—

the one who needs it.

DELICATE QUESTION

I spit in your eye, my purulent Europe,
and ask the question:

What are you so proud of?

Is it your sanatoriums in the mountains,
crammed full of tuberculotics
or your brothels
in which hundreds of thousands are infected?
Is it your coal mines,
where men suffocate from gas
or your war industry,
which is truly developed, first rate?

What are you so proud of?

Your feudal castles perhaps,
where serfs were flogged for centuries,
or your salaried communist agitators?
Is it your youth,
who play politicking with live ammunition,
or your gynecologists
who make an excellent living from abortions?

So what is it that you're so proud of?
You pale, toothless, white men's procuress, Europe,
you old hag.

Your pseudo-culture will be clogged with the rot
of your own muck,
which the chimneys of your factories retch upward

to the height of twenty storeys,
and as Troy was rebuilt on the ruins of six cities
and then destroyed a seventh time by war,
so will a new world be built
over your seven-times-destroyed parliaments—
a world whose citizens
will not only be concerned
with foreign policy and taxation.

WORLD HISTORY

I was a dictator in my infancy,
(if I cried,
no one could sleep
because of me)

later on
I did give some of the chocolate
to my little brother,

which is definitely a sign of constitution.

In school
we fought every day.
(Republic. Divine human rights.)

And when my voice
started to change:

anarchy raged in me.

Since then, I lived through
several revolutions:

my own illusions beheaded me—

and now,
here I stand,
without a form of government:

just as
did once—

   prehistoric man.

TYPEWRITER

the poet who now speaks
is the 1913 type, portable,
still in quite good shape

and soundlessly
pours out the lines
for adult and children's magazines

as we can see, he is a relatively
new model,
the capital letters, however,
can no longer be made to work

contrary to his convictions,
without full stop or exclamation mark,
he is compelled
to write only small-letter things

in red,
if a red ribbon is inserted,
if it is black, he writes in black

but sometimes,
in the middle of the night,
without paper or ribbon

he taps upon
invisible ghostly lines

at such times, the neighbours
object furiously
to the nocturnal disturbance of peace

but a girl who
is in love with him
says of him

that he is writing poems

THE COIN

Have you ever thought what it's like
for a flat-footed door-to-door salesman
in the concrete jungle without insteps?
But do you also realize
that those same flat feet, in time of war,
may mean life?

The coin, as you can see,
has two sides,
and a person can only see one side at a time.
So don't imagine that you are a paragon of virtue
just because, being a clerk at the mint, you do not
    embezzle—
because, had you been the killer in the armed hold-up in
    the city,
it isn't certain that you wouldn't have done it out of
    sheer despair.
So he is right
who defends himself in court,
and so is the prosecutor who accuses him
and the lawyer who defends him,
and so, too, is the judge who hands down the death
    penalty.
Because we are all human beings
who only ever see one side of the coin,
and even if there are a handful among us
who resort to higher contemplation—
they stand on the edge of the coin,
so do not see either side.

THE SEEDSMAN

The man turned grey.
Though his hair was still glistening black,
his longings were already snow-white.
"Life is no longer worthwhile," he sighed
and set off to the valley of tranquility.

Death was harvesting in the valley.
Big-eared stalks fell under his blows,
then he saw the man,
and he asked him:

"What have you accomplished?"

The man stopped and replied:

"I was a seedsman,
I scattered the seeds of my body
among women.
I added flavor to fertility.
If a woman was thirsty for kisses,
I let her drink from my own blood,
if a girl yearned for secrets,
I showed them on her body.
There were no barren flowers left
along my path,
blooming was the branch that sprung from my body.

I was once a seedsman,
but my desires have withered since."

He hung his head and waited.

"You were a poor manager," said death,
"sowed your seeds into fertile soil
and then neglected them.

Go, tend to your seedlings!"

The man went back on the road,
and death continued
its relentless harvest.

OBLIGATORY SPRING POEM

Ars poetica for the weather- and water-level-reporting poets

Spring

yesterday obtained
the majority of the shares in Time,
and I,
as my feelings'
domestic servant:

had already today
spring-cleaned
in my soul.

I started
the cost price clearance
of my remaining thoughts
from winter

and promptly noted down
a few original thoughts
to summer.

By the way, I hope
that this autumn, too,
the trees will shed

the yellowed leaves

and that around December
will fall
the title of my winter poem:

"The First Snowflake."

BUDAPEST DIVISION

All told, we just wanted to be people,
but we shall become compulsory reading—

and in twelfth grade, during history class,
the teacher will explain about us—
just as
       on the basis
       of the high school syllabus
another history teacher talked to us once

about the breakthrough at Gorlic:

"Grenades were falling,
charge upon charge, one following the other,
and from a battalion of a thousand men
perhaps not even twenty stayed alive,
still no retreating, boys,

for the Budapest Division."

It's peacetime now, you say, a trifle alarmed,
and at the movies you console yourself,

but believe that this front line
is already invisibly connected.
In vain does the one carry coal on his back;
the other sits in a luxury car in vain,
in a factory, workshop, or in the office;
in vain do you have flat feet or an acid stomach,

destiny—will carve you: from human into hero!

Now they call you Steve, possibly Sam,
you have your own name, your worries and your life,
but by degrees you'll become a 'concept',

your fate: mass grave,
your rank: heroic dead,
and instead of Steve, one day
they'll call you

the Budapest Division.

All told, we just wanted to be people,
you, a writer, he, a shop assistant,

and now, with a pen or a paper bag in our hands,
not one amongst us understands:

why will we become
history?
And why will the teacher explain
in twelfth grade, during history class,
that we were born to be heroes

    —with minor bodily flaws—

you and I.

IN THE LAST FEW DAYS

I've been so engrossed in myself
that the girl I am going with
is desperately jealous of me

and because of me.

Just yesterday, when, for example,
I was rushing on the street somewhere
so as not to be late,

I looked at my watch

and unexpectedly asked myself:
who is this strange young man
who holds my briefcase
in his hand
and rushes in my trench coat
and in my skin
towards his momentary goal.

Unfortunately, there was not one acquaintance
coming towards me
whom I could have asked,

so I stopped and sat down on a bench
because all of a sudden
this had become most important for me.

Good Lord, I thought, frightened,
I run around here on earth,
I went to school,
I have a degree,

and now I'm learning to play the piano—
why this great fervor
to get to know different things
and other people?

Then, as with a puzzle solver
who surmounts the last obstacle,
it flashed before me:

that every effort we make
to get to know others
is only for the purpose
of finally getting a little closer

to ourselves.

OVER THE SPEED OF 100 KILOMETERS

Hit the pedal, 20th Century, my big chauffeur,
don't be concerned that lying in wait for us is the horror
    of speed:
the mental puncture.
We live in an age
when owing to aeroplanes the trees will in no way grow
    to the sky,
so rev it to the utmost, and let's rush ahead.
What will be—will be!

Who cares whether
a new renaissance can be created out of concrete,
or if a machine can produce
motherly love.
Don't question a thing. Business—is Business!
Below Chief Executive, use the back stairs, please.

Why would you care about another
when you can't kick him so hard
that you wouldn't be kicking yourself.
Let everyone shout themselves hoarse,
a Bosch horn will outscream them all.

Don't question a thing.
In America they ran a competition
for an over-sixteen-year-old girl who's still a virgin,
and for lack of entrants
it was won by a young man from Boston.

That's all!
Whether civilization stands or falls is not important:
today, for cash, you can get

chewing gum, streetwalkers and courtesy
in instalments,
well-brought-up girls, trench coats and His Master's
    Voice gramophones—

and a young Italian engineer invented:
the wireless embrace.

BLOOD PACT

I am the pact in blood!

My Father made it with my Mother,
and this alliance
is stronger

than any
Ancient or New Alliance.

My Mother's blood
was

the ink,

God struck

the seal
    (hard birth,
    drenched in sweat),

and it was my Father
who

signed it.

My body is this
strange document,

but, oh, what would happen
if I were

to tear it apart.

LOST GENERATION

Of late I've often wondered:
why am I a lost generation?

Probably, because,
while in the prewar years
a young man's sole ambition was
to secure a job with a government pension,

among my most daring dreams is—
a fatal traffic accident.

Then I, too, would finally make a career—
and my mother would also have some benefit out of me,
        the car is a dangerous machine,
        she would definitely receive
        compensation,
and I am absolutely certain
that I would also figure in the politicians' pronouncements,
        "We have finally succeeded in solving
        the problem of youth unemployment."

I'm afraid, though,
that not even this dream of mine can be fulfilled,
because there are still
too many young men—
        and too few cars.

I have not yet decided, but it is possible that tomorrow
I'll put a classified
in one of the bigger morning papers:

LOST: THE MEANING OF MY LIFE!
between 1913 and 1937.

I appeal to the honest finder
to keep the whole affair a secret
because someone could well report him to the police
for hiding a spy in his apartment:

who, when one day he finds himself before God,
will reveal everything about what he saw and
experienced

down there on Earth.

MECHANICAL PRAYER

Nowadays, man no longer respects
the legally registered patent
of the World-Creating God,
and, measuring devotion with horse power,
he's trying to blow God's body to smithereens
with a force of ten million volts.

My Lord—why do You allow it?
Little by little man will turn into a machine,
and the machines will not be able to pray to You.

Look,
the chicks are already being hatched by machines,
and one fine day the machine will give birth to man,
who will orbit on his path with mathematical accuracy,
and a power failure will be the cause of his death.

So why did You create us?
Since the time will come
when babies will suck petrol
from communal pumps
in place of mother's milk,
because the chemically-produced infants
will have no need
for such emotional family interactions.

I bow my head and murmur to myself:

"... Your kingdom come ..."—
but by then man will be a formula
in which, if you substitute Your eternal design,
he will live out his life without rebellion—

and just as You had once created him from dust,
just so he will turn to rust.

HAPPINESS

Across seven continents I searched for you far and wide.

I turned into a fish for you
and measured the depth of the oceans,
then catching an aeroplane
I measured my own height in a department store,
and just as I thought I'd never find you,
I realized that I had left you in the hallway.

Inside, the landlady for whom I lusted over the years
served up dinner and her body,
and when I parted from her,
I was missing you again.

I tried to remain near you,
but I was only getting further and further away,
and when I got too far away,
I was compelled to buy a transfer ticket.

Just then, I had a capital idea—
decided to become a movie star
and, having put a friendly face to the Soviet system of
    agriculture,
I drilled the bottom of the Atlantic Ocean,
hoping that
just for once you would get caught
in the torn net of my fate.

At that point the water refused to seep through the net
and I, having lost my causal connection,
read an uncut version of *The Blue Bird*
and discovered what I had long suspected:
that it dyes its feathers.

POEM OF THE UNEMPLOYED

My chosen judges—the clock that hangs on the wall,
the framed Gobelin and the ashtray,
assembled to judge my case.

"Gentlemen of the jury," said I, and bowed low
towards the bookshelf where my jurors:

Renan's, Merezhkovsky's and Mikszáth's works
sat in hardback.

"I am accused,
though being of age,
of never yet having earned my keep!

Regrettably, the charge brought against me
is true, what's more, I also have to confess
that I lead a distinctly wasteful lifestyle:

my pulse beats sixty-six times per minute,
so if I were to deduct six from this
I would not even need a second hand
on my pocket watch,

but I do not bother myself even with that."

"And you are guaranteed to be disappointed,"
I continued heatedly, "if you think I have a watch.
Oh, I pawned it long ago, and anyway
I can honestly say that not even
gold watches interest me,
since it is common knowledge
that I squander the day."

My chosen judges looked at each other,
and the jurors were also perplexed—in hardback,

and then the clock on the wall began to speak :
    tic-toc,
    who are you actually,
    tic-toc,
    accused, accuser
    or accusation.

KEY POEM

Before you write a love poem, young man,
do some physiological research
on guinea pigs
at the Institute of Life Sciences—
because love is a mysterious room
whose key is: the woman!

The door will not open,
nor will the house of pleasures,
if the woman doesn't want it.

So all the way for her!
Though, for a couple of bucks, the janitor's duplicate
will open a door for anyone.

But that's not the real key—
for the real key
one has to suffer,
just as She will suffer, when, like a key
turning in the lock,
through the open door
you receive:

your child!

NOW I CONFESS

I would've liked
to have been like God:
a bachelor,
solitary, single being
without woman, child
and the whole baggage,
free to follow
my heart's desire.

But I now know

that it's easy to be God
without woman, child
and the whole baggage,
never, never
needing to think
of a mouth hungry
for a slice bread.

And now I sense
my life's purpose:

all of humanity
are members of my family,

hunger, worry
and sorrow

are my illegitimate, but true children.

AT THE TOMB OF THE UNKNOWN SOLDIER

We have come to you, Unknown Soldier,
we, the last groans of the World War's fallen heroes,
who for the sake of protecting our common interests
merged into a cartel,
have come to tell you
that we haven't vanished into thin air.
We've come to tell you here and now
that up above
nowadays people think of you only in terms of statistics,
and they are erecting multi-storied obelisks
over their tumultuous consciences.
We've come to you,
20,000,000th heroic dead,
so cited in every memorial speech,
because those who made the war
know that
20,000,000 strangers don't amount to
one dead father.
We've come to you,
we, who know that every one of you
singularly experienced the horror of death,
and only in the raise-your-glasses toasts
are you an indifferent 20,000,000.
We, the last groans of the World War's fallen heroes,
who for the sake of protecting our common interests
merged into a cartel,
have come to tell you
that we haven't vanished into thin air—
but the atmosphere of our world
has long been surrounded
by toxic gases.

ACCOMPLICES

Since yesterday morning
I refuse to be on a first-name basis
with myself,

but even this
is an unnecessary civility.

Such a lying scoundrel,
who for years fed me promises
and raised so many futile hopes in me,
he should be glad
that I speak to him at all.

But I do only because,
if things go badly for a person,
he lives off the interest
of his pleasant memories,

but if he has no memories
and still wants to endure life,
then he must forgo
the gold standard of reality

for unsecured dream currency.

So if the truth be known, we are accomplices:
he, the instigator, and I, the culprit—

but while he, the hardened criminal,
routinely misappropriates

reality—

only by coercion
am I a fence for my pipe dreams.

PARLIAMENTARIANISM

Yesterday was the first time I met you:

today, there is already a government crisis
in my heart,
and you are

the prime minister designate.

The right
is receiving the news with reservation

because my wallet is on that side,

but you lean on the left

because you know
that I wear my heart there.

Your program:

exactly the same
as that of your predecessor;

you, too, promise
what you can't keep;

but if your budget
also resembles hers,
I will be compelled to declare

bankruptcy.

EXPEDITION

I am not interested in Mount Everest,
the secrets of the South Pole
or the Gobi Desert—
for me, the only and truly
unknown territory
is: You.
Rouge on the faces of other women,
silk dresses on their bodies,
manicure on their hands
are like the promotion campaign
of the Bureau of Foreign Travel,
with which they aim to entice the tourist.
But You are missing from
Baedeker's *Guides*,
intended for strangers,
because You have not yet been mapped.
The Wall of China surrounds You,
emanating from your being,
and while
suitable expedition equipment
for reaching the others is:
a car, a gold chain
or twenty bucks,
no road nor path leads to You,
and only
the magic carpet of the spirit helps.
You are sitting beside me,
yet still extraordinarily far,
and my hand, which is so famous
from successes in other expeditions
that it could well be a member
of the British Royal Geographic Society,

now hesitates next to Your body
like the polar explorer,
enchanted for the first time
by the—over-the-unknown-terrain-
coolly-radiating—

Northern light.

MOMENTS

My finger,

as if it were the big hand of the clock,
I lay upon your breast,
and in the silence of the night
I listen
to how mysteriously is ticking
the wonder-wrought timepiece of our love—
your heart.

Oh—because the moments are passing—

and with every drop of blood
that courses through your heart,
people fall to the ground,

and while we, with our kisses,
greet life in advance,

upon another's pulse
politely knocks

death.

AND IF IT SADDENS YOU

... and if it saddens you now and then
that the majority is always right,

just think that the wise wedded gods of antiquity
were already in the minority

compared with prolific humanity.

Likewise, the stories of Goodness and Human Intelligence
could fit into a single book,
whereas the stories of wickedness and of man's stupidity
need libraries—

you see, that's why
there are so few really good books on earth

and so many public libraries
at the expense of the public purse!

ART GALLERY

My soul is a public art gallery,
but in it
there is a private room
where
aside from me

for strangers entry—is strictly forbidden. In the other
halls anyone can hang their picture, I cannot verify
whether it is a forgery
or the original—

   but in here

there is silence and rapture
and a few etchings

   of my dead father,
   my mother,
   and you

just—as I see each of you:

after my own heart—free-hand.

MUSIC FOR PROSE

Your body is an Aeolian harp,
and I have played upon it:

the most beautiful melodies of my life.

The feverish passages
have subsided,
but when I leave home,
I frequently notice
that

I'm humming
the refrain of our love.

Oh, I know so well:

there is music elsewhere,
screeching, unbridled cacophony
emitted towards me
by many strange women,

but more than
by every strange counterpoint,
I am enchanted

by the rhythm of your giving.

The concert of my youth
is over!

And of my desires,
composed for a full orchestra,
came a quartet:

my son, my daughter, you and my mother.

And now instead of the XIth symphony
(in which I set to score
the other women)

I conduct that melody

in the manner in which,
with the slow movement of your hips,
you cradle your newborn.

FAMILY EVENT

Our potted palm
sprouted a new branch
by the morning.

The cyclamens
inquisitively surrounded

the newborn.
"We had a hard night,"
said the corn leaf.

"You can say that again,
I cannot tell you how many times I thought
that it would all turn out badly,"
added officiously—
an asparagus.

But as things stand,
we thank you for your kind inquiry,
mother and child
are doing fine.

    "How tiny,
    and already how green!"

Of course, you can tell just by looking at him
what a distinguished family
he comes from.

Because, if I may say:

on his mother's side
he can trace his family tree
all the way back to the Sahara.

You know,
that is where those
mighty palm trees are found

among whom,
translated into human terms,
even the puniest is

at the very least
an Undersecretary of State.

Mr. Neighbor,
haven't you heard yet?
Our palm gave birth to a little boy
during the night!

And I don't even know why,
but I am so nervous ...

Tell me, what do you think?

Shouldn't we tell the janitor
not to let the tenants do
any carpet-beating at all today?

They are just capable
of waking up

the little one.

PHILOSOPHICALLY PROFOUND POEM

Give me a firm spot in space,
and I will build the first
five-hundred-room aircastle with hot and cold running
    water,
where for a daily two hundred dollars
even the poorest person gets
a cosy, soft, warm and
friendly handshake.
Because it's not the pan-European ideals I want to realize,
my obsession is—
that if it be utopia, at least it should be edible.
Yes—because, more important than any bridge problem is
that there are people on earth
whose reason for not eating meat every day
is not on account of a medical diet
but because,
regrettably, the butcher and small-goods industries
are only geared toward short-term loans,
and so they don't even give twenty grams of bacon rind for
the saying:
... may God repay you ...
    Unfortunately, in the great depression God-shares have
hit rock bottom,
and people sell to one another the very air for cash,
not to mention—that for cash they are also willing to
withhold it from one another.
So this is where the preachings and the Culberston-style
contract bridge played among friends
has gotten them.
The whole world, like a crazed and naked whore,
turns itself into small change,

so that, having subsequently
drugged its self-awareness
with fashionable fads and poisons—
it would not hear
the dull, monotonous heartbeats
of the wretched troops of the hungry—
which, with rhythmic protractions, burn
into their parched brains

the new murders'
and the new wars'
triumphant, all-consuming hatred.

MEMORIAL SPEECH

Charles Robert Darwin,
the ringside referee of the fist fight of the races,
lives in the parish cemetery of Downe—
was born in Shrewsbury
by the grace of God and from his own mother,
as is generally the custom
among mammals.
Already in his youth,
with great love, he turned
to the natural sciences,
because he, too, had noticed
what others tried to deny.
At the conclusion of his studies
he wandered extensively among primitive peoples
but later discovered
that, gentlemen's fashions notwithstanding,
the struggle for survival
was eminently observable
in London—
and precisely for this reason settled down
in England.
African memories threw him into temptation
when he dared to call the consumptive pariahs
of the English coal mines
relatives of the free, brave and giant gorillas—
so that this error,
which caused a potent uproar
in the whole of the animal kingdom,
even among the sheep and yoke-pulling cattle,
may be forgiven him.
At the end of his life,

as he felt his last hour approaching,
in accordance with the right of every free, tax-paying
English citizen,
he died—
and with that extraordinary act of his,
having created an even greater furor
in the whole of the cultured world
than did his theories—

as is right and proper,
he arrived amongst the immortals.

MR. SOMOGYI, OR THE EVERYDAY ODE

"Mr. Somogyi," I said to him
as we turned into the boulevard
            the wind howled in our faces—
            shivering, I buttoned up my coat
            and the electric clock showed
            half past one in the morning
"Mr. Somogyi—twice already you've had
gallstones, and once, for three weeks,
you were held in jail under investigation,

tell me, what is the meaning of our lives?"

"I know that now you think me crazy," I continued
as he looked at my face in amazement—
            he had such colorless eyes
            that when he applied for
            his passport, the police clerk,
            in his embarrassment, didn't know
            what color to write in
"because this I should really be asking God,
since only He can answer it,

but God is so far away, Mr. Somogyi,
and I don't have any gate money;
I am hoping to borrow twenty cents from you—
And whosoever helps us out of our immediate money
     crises

—always amounts a little to God—

that is why I turn to you, Mr. Somogyi,
with my question, aside from my petition."

Somogyi was mutely silent,
        because it is possible to be talkatively silent;
        the neon sign on the façade of the house
        at Octagon Square was also silent,
        and still it brazenly roared
        towards us:
        Moulin Rouge, Moulin Rouge
and he was embarrassed because he couldn't answer.

"Can it be possible, Mr. Somogyi,
that we only live for life's pleasures?
But surely, life's pleasures spring from life—
without life, there wouldn't be any aim,
without life, we wouldn't have—our lives?"

"You see that broad coming towards us?"
asked Somogyi with a sly glance,
"she's a good lay, and I'll pay for you
as well because you're a decent young man,
and I like being with you, just don't
ask me such idiocies like—the tax form ..."
        and he looked at me reprehensively.

"You are right," I answered with a sinking heart.
"Mr. Somogyi, you are absolutely right,
after all, what is the meaning of meaning?

If we do it cleverly enough,
the satisfaction of our senses
can provide us
with sufficient local desensitization,

it doesn't matter therefore
whether they call it lust, belief,

wine or opium—
all we need to watch out for
is that, in the balancing of our existence,

the scale shouldn't tilt in our minds' favor
        because *blessed are the poor in spirit,*
Mr. Somogyi, who do not question, who only eat
and who, for those very reasons,
even from the point of view of governability,
are above reproach
        and *theirs is the Kingdom of Heaven,*

with free first-class tickets
all the way
to the gates of Saint Peter."

I WAS ABOUT FIFTEEN YEARS OLD

when I caught the illness
every healthy young man gets:

I wanted to redeem
suffering humanity.

Only God truly knows,
how high my fever rose

when I saw a sick person
or an old beggar.

Then Hitler came and the years passed—
the fever turned into constant temperature
—but I am still among the living!

And when, a convalescent,
I walk on the street

my young dreams still
wave to me from afar,
the trees and the flowers
greet me with a secret sign.

And wherever I go
the old gas lamps look gratefully
up to the sky
and give thanks
that after so many brown shirts—

a human being has finally
    walked by.

PEACE

Tra-raa, Tra-raa, Tra-raa,
sounded the trumpets,
the radios, and the loudspeakers bellowed,
and the billposters proclaimed:
    people no longer said to each other
    Good Morning, Bonjour,
    Heil Hitler, Evviva Mussolini,
    and they no longer raised
    their arms in greeting;
    instead, with bowed heads
    they mumbled the new kind of salute—

GENERAL MOBILISATION!

And the shepherds came from the mountains,
    and they were drafted,
the fishermen came from the banks of rivers,
    and they were drafted,
the hunters came from the depths of forests,
    and they were drafted.
In their wake, on mountain and on meadow
soared a liberated chant:

PEACE, PEACE, PEACE—sang the birds,
game and fish rejoiced—
at last, peace has moved in amongst us!

People will not hurt us any more
because from now on people

will hunt each other.

A POET, HIS SOUL IN WHITE TIE AND TAILS

A poet, his soul in white tie and tails,
lacking any means of income
stands here in the middle of Europe,

he can't even afford to repay
the debt he owes his mother
for years of raising him.

Hm, nice world we live in!
Or perhaps you have some biblical quotation
for this as well?

What's your opinion about a Modern Evangelism
that would worry a trifle about one's stomach?

A poet whose head and limbs
stick out from his soul's garb
like a turtle's from its shell

stands here and wonders
why they're so concerned about his soul
instead of worrying about his limbs,

which will definitely be in need,
unlike his head,

in case of war.

100% POEM

Only 5% for the mood you're in,

the heart, the feeling
or something else 5%

the other 95
is compulsory tax

morality must
reverberate out of you

(even between friends .... 20%)

so that you can slip by
the censor:

must sacrifice another 45-ish

the editor
who accepts you
requires
his own percentage 20%

and printing errors
will still amount to,
give or take, a 10-er

This is how you'll turn into a 100%
war-wounded poem

or a heroic dead.

MANHOOD

Till now, every woman
was my sweetheart,
if not in deed—

at least in thought,

but now I'm a man,
I have to work,
and I don't have much time
to daydream.

Yet how interesting it was,

sometimes for months on end
I hadn't bed
a woman

but in my little-boy body
in minutes
I lived through
the amorous delights of generations.

By now, I don't have
illusions anymore,

just a monthly pass
to a little house—
whose name
changes
according to social class.

And these days:

I also meet
genteel girls,
even
reputable women—

but with them one better be
careful

because you could easily end up
paying child support.

THE DREAM

From their daily bread
he broke off half
    and then decided
    that for the purposes of propaganda
he would hire their dreams as well.

And the next day, when the workers
went to the factory,
this is what they read on the notice boards:

    Do not wallow
    in your fantasy-rich dreams!
    Dream about the main and by-products
    of the Oxygen Works Ltd.
    Dream about oxygen, hydrogen,
    nitrogen and carbon monoxide.
    Dream about the products of our subsidiary
    —mustard gas and chlorine gas—
    dream about oxidation,
    but, categorically, dream only in connection
    with The Oxygen Works Ltd.!

And the workers, who lived off air,
now not only gave their nights and days to the factory
but spent their dreams with it as well.

Not much later the foremen
ran to the Chief Executive
in desperation.

"Our Leader! A young worker is dreaming about Ozone
and could not care less
about the Oxygen Works."

"Bring him to me immediately."
They ran for him, and brought
the worker at once.

"Is it true what they are saying about you?"

"Yes. I dream whatever I please.
After all,
    my dream—is my dream,"
    he emphasized it in the same way as
    Monroe once said that
    America belongs to Americans.
"And anyway," he added,
"it is not included in the collective contract
that everyone must dream
in accordance with factory regulations."

"I kick you out," roared the Chief. "I kick out
the collective contract, and I'll kick
myself out if it serves the interests of the company.
Do you understand?"

The worker was intelligent, and in front of the factory
he touched himself gingerly where they had kicked him
    out,
then he went into town.
A few weeks later, alarming news came
from the direction of the town.

Like they said: the worker established
The Society of Dreamers Independent of Factory
    Regulations,
he created their rallying tune and
is organizing resistance outside the trade union.
The foremen rushed to the Chief again:

"Our Leader! Someone is smuggling
revolutionary powder to the workers.
It is being made by the worker who was kicked out
and by a young chemist.
Whoever takes this powder
not only does not dream anymore
but ceases to think as well."

"What?" exclaimed the Chief Executive in amazement.
"If that is how it is," he added with tears in his eyes,
"then go for him
and bring him here—in my place,
and I'll resign,
because he is your true man.
Hosanna to him."

Thus spoke the Chief Executive of the Oxygen Works Ltd.
And on hearing such magnanimous generosity
even the workers with the most revolutionary disposition
were touched and long waved
their kerchiefs after the former Chief Executive's
disappearing Rolls Royce.

This story is about a worker who rebelled
so that he could become Chief Executive.
Let the so-called self-awareness of the working masses
    mourn him.
But his relatives are not nearly as sad.
If someone should inquire about the moral of this story
    with you,
modify Napoleon's words a little—like this:
Every proletaire carries in his purse the dream,

the dream
that one day he also will become a capitalist.

THE 10,000,001st LOVE POEM IN PROSE

Thus far approximately 10,000,000 love poems have been written by poets! They compared the eyes of the beloved to sapphires, the ocean, the dawn, what's more, a futurist poet said: "Your eyes are like the shade of the mulberry tree"—*why the shade of the walnut tree wasn't suitable for the same purpose, I will never know, but I fear that this may well remain one of the major problems of my life.*

Since, based on the title of my poem, I too am compelled to express an opinion about your eyes—in my embarrassment I can only say: you have quite nice eyes—like a woman's eyes.

I hope that, although this simile of mine is excessively daring and incomprehensible, they will not declare me a Cubist poet.

Your mouth resembles neither rubies nor grapes nor amaranth and, in parentheses, I'd indelicately add that with the same mouth every so often you eat spring onions —naturally, only when they're in season, otherwise the brown ones will do.

Your neck is somewhat thicker than a swan's, but, let it be said to your advantage, it's also that much shorter.

About your breasts, regrettably, I cannot write anything —I haven't yet had the good fortune of meeting them intimately, only like this, through your blouse, but I shouldn't think that they were made either from marble or bronze, or that they resemble ripe apples, because I know that you're far more practical not to have boasted about them long ago.

Your waist—I'm compelled to say—is a thousand times wider than a bee's, although you do Swedish exercises, unlike it.

Your legs are as slender as a deer's, I say this with the unknown songwriter in mind; it's just that your feet are man-size.

Regarding your hands, I must admit I can't say anything original, because such hands are worn by two billion people, with the difference that not all of them are gloved in deerskin, but frequently in lighter shades of imitation.

I left your shoulders to the last because they're utterly sensational and modern: square. Say, can you imagine round shoulders, like in the past—weird.

I think I've succeeded in sketching your figure, though I feel that, carried away by my feverish fantasy, I was at times too unrealistic. Now I'll go further. Your soul is like a white sheet—no one would believe how dirty it was before wash day—though you are clean, and wash frequently. You are good and you give to beggars, because you know that men like the woman who gives her all.

You are not a spendthrift and you save your own—I wouldn't say that you do the same with mine, though given the economy, you would hardly find much to spend from it.

You love children. Just the other day, after you saw me walking with Maggie, you said: "You don't even know what a sweet little boy Maggie has." Weren't you by any chance referring to her unmarried status?

... And yet, always, I waited for you only. For you I waited and searched with tear-filled eyes. I would have liked to kiss your footprints, but, alas, footprints are not visible on asphalt.

It's as if I sensed your fragrance, which is more intoxicating than the smell of wild flowers in the meadow. I saw before me your hair's shiny softness, your lips, upon which desire crimsons with feverish restlessness, the silky pink bloom of your face, and the poster:

ELIDA: powder, perfume, rouge and shampoo.

ORPHAN POEM

Your mother: was yesterday's mood,
your father: a fleeting instant,

even if I take pity on you
and bring you up,
you'll remain a foundling, my little one.

You might even cause me embarrassment—

if a banker were to ask:
Mr. Poet, what did you do yesterday
between twelve noon and half past—

because I must confess that during that time
I made a hundred thousand dollars.

Or how would I answer
if, having been accused of murder,
a relentless prosecutor with piercing eyes
were to question:

what did you do on that same day
between twelve noon and half past?

And what should my answer be
if they were to ask me up there about
what I did down here on earth?

It's not yet conclusive, but I might say:

down there, I lived among bloodletting and hatred,
but I was not an accomplice to any wrongdoing,

and recall that I once wrote
an orphan poem—

this, too, could corroborate me before You—my God.

God, upon hearing this curious alibi,
would doubtless smile,
and at dawn, on a summer day,
would surely endorse
my having been a poet.

TAKING A BIRD'S EYE VIEW OF MY LIFE

Taking a bird's eye view of my life
I feel that

it's but the struggle of vanity,
like
two gloves
in the hand of a one-armed cavalier.

Bit by bit, my heart is
like blotting paper:

though it soaks up every experience,
everything also runs together on it.

And I really can't help it
if, like a semaphore, my grey eye
constantly shows:
Verboten!

as if wanting to signal
that the train of my life

is sidelined on open tracks.

I LIKE YOUNG, FIRM, ROUND BREASTS

I like young, firm, round breasts,
but I know that Rembrandt was of a different opinion,
and for this very reason, gentlemen,
I'm willing to acknowledge
that tastes differ.
     Yes—tastes do differ,
but it's hard to fathom one
that only a World War would satisfy.
Or else why didn't they continue
the war until the last person had perished,
why must humanity be slowly driven crazy
and annihilated piecemeal.
My intention is entirely honorable;
and the reason I wrote
such a titillating first sentence was
to entice Man to read
that vis-à-vis Truth we are
like the proverbial person with a toothache
who always has the healthy tooth extracted.
Because it's undeniable
that they always do something
in the name of Truth,
just not what needs to be done.
So, gentlemen, barons and assorted gypsy lads,
why do we struggle to stay alive
once we're in the here and now?
     Well, just so as to live
and not have to die young,
because whilst it's true that life begins
at a fixed income of 400,
I would still rather be a living unemployed
than a dead landlord.

THE LAST SPECTATOR

On earth everyone was already a movie star.

In the Great Dictionary of the Academy,
in place of the word 'Heaven', 'Hollywood' appeared.
Nightly, throughout the whole world,
artificial smoke clouds concealed the starry sky,
and instead of a movie screen
the program was projected onto the milky, white clouds.

The male children were christened Valentino
or Clark Gable,
Greta Garbo's statue stood in every city's main square,
and in the telephone books
for every Smith there were 10,000 Barrymores.

And mothers-to-be, under threat of monetary fines,
were compelled by the authorities
in the last months of their blessed state
to more and more diligently frequent
the movies of Robert Taylor and Ginger Rogers

so that their about-to-be-born children would also
be that beautiful.

In the schools they no longer taught
the Cosine theory,
instead, as a compulsory exercise everywhere on earth
every day, for two hours, high school students worked in
     laboratories
on the manufacture of heatable and scented film.
And people from every part of the globe
poured into the British Museum,
in whose film section

a couple in love, petrified while kissing
could be viewed,

and on the accompanying plaque only this much was
  stated:

THIS IS HOW THE MOVIES ENDED—AROUND 1940!

At the movies, the audience had become completely
  unnecessary.
People willingly bought tickets
to every movie
just so they wouldn't have to see it
because everyone knew the films' contents ahead of
  time
since the committee only allowed
those films past censorship

which, for every cubic meter of talking,
colored and plastic film, contained:

  more than 0.567 cubic decimeters of being in love,
  11.28 cubic centimeters of Berlin blue,
  and 129.43 cubic millimeters of the hair-raising—

and anyway,
(as in the past with rayon or linen),
every better retailer kept a stock of film stories,
from the Grand Guignol to the Burlesque,
and although women had these turned into dresses,
an experienced film director or a seamstress who came in
made quite a tolerable movie out of them
for home use, provided they bought with it another
10 decagrams of Gags.

The last spectator, whom the leading motion picture studios
    studios
contracted for an exorbitant sum
for the purpose of viewing their films
was a photocell
which expressed its approval with light signals
under the influence of artistic achievements,

        emitted ultra violet rays
        from itself

and, if the movie was not liked,

automatically disconnected itself—

        and so, let us confess, was far more perfect
        than a spectator in 1938,
        who could never give expression
        to his dislike by leaving the movie theater
        half way through the projection
        because the rows of chairs were narrow
        and the overharassed people, instead of feet,
        already only wore corns in their shoes,
        and after all, just because he was bored
        with the thing,
        he couldn't disturb his fellow humans'
        happy and satisfied dreams

        when all through the night they couldn't sleep
           anyway
        because of their worries.

I SENTENCE MY SELF-ESTEEM TO LIFELONG LIFE

Following this concentration of my equity,
I'll put the remaining tiny fraction towards
sewing dolls' dresses for the unemployed lilies of the
    field,
and I await the prince of fairy tales—
whose bankruptcy was declared yesterday—
to take me on mass-produced dream clouds
of quiet winter evenings
to a job with a secure salary,
because by now I know that
better a sparrow today
than its carrion tomorrow,
since I had been to the funeral of an undertaker,
and I have a friend who was born in the light of day
and is now a jobless nightwatchman.

It is exactly for this reason that I'd like to obtain
the qualifications of Chief Executive,
but, alas, at the Polytechnic of Selfishness and
    Indifference
they rejected my application, claiming that
I still harbor too many social sentiments.

So, these days I spend my time
slowly killing off all feelings of humanism,
and since my progress in this area
is extremely promising,
I hope that soon I'll become
my country's leading taxpayer
and respected pillar of society.

WHOLESALING

The year was 1914, and America sent cars, grain and
    chewing gum.
The year was 1915, and America sent canned meat,
    boots and dollars.
The year was 1916, and America sent aeroplanes and
    curious tourists.
The year was 1917, trench warfare, and America sent
    soldiers.
The year was 1918 and America sent gold, English
pounds, liras, zloyts, francs and Deutsche marks back to
    America.

And in the meantime, in New York, each day new deals
were made on the Stock Exchange,
and the trains in Pennsylvania ran on time.

In the Follies you could see sketches of the war,
and in Russia the soldiers froze,
and in Germany they died,
and in France they were wounded:
... and America continued to transport!
Scrap metal, nurses, diversions for the soldiers at the
    front,
light bulbs and door knobs,
bandages, jeans and
philanthropy,
films, white bread,
and thermoses,
torch batteries, odorless gas,
and Red Cross packages.

And afterwards, when the whole stupid comedy was over,
and when at last 10,000,000 people had perished
it packed up the last pillow
pulled from under Europe's head,
decked out New York City with flags, went home:
    and won the World War.

STAR

Sometimes I imagine
that I'm a star,

then I quickly
talk myself out of it
because there's absolutely nothing

I could orbit around.

Yet how good would it be
to be a star:

I could stay out every night,
at least until dawn,
and during a downpour,
from behind the boudoir screens of the clouds

I too could impertinently gatecrash
Earth.

Wouldn't that be something!

Still, being a star must have its problems—
at our place we only use 40-watt light bulbs,
yet our electricity bill

is still a headache.

How much more could a star
be paying?

And anyway,
I've long known
that there's no Heaven—

so then why would I advertise it
in such bright lights?

I'M ONLY DISSIPATING ENERGY

and one day
I'll be smaller
than the smallest dot,

so minute

as to be
ultramicroscopic.

Then they'll call me
the Infinite,

and I'll be a member
of the Orchestra of Spheres,

and if we feel like it,
my siblings, the ether waves, and I
will gaily roam

in the Great Void,

and none of us
will give a thought
that
meanwhile
down on Earth,

there had been spring, summer, autumn
and armistice.

FOR TWO DOLLARS, COME ON IN, SWEETIE

we promise you heavenly pleasures
with an emotional turn-on or however you like it.
Trust me, money is an equalizer,
and we are the world's only true socialists
because for a trifling sum
we treat banker and sewage worker
exactly alike.

For all this, we don't in advance
require a blood test, romantic movies
or dyspeptic mushiness.

We do double-entry bookkeeping,
accurately deducting the deductable
because we know
that money speaks and the unemployed barks,
but the barking doesn't reach
Managing Directors' ears.

So don't believe in interest-free love
and support the home industry
because whosoever can still believe in an idea
can, for a paltry two dollars,
become a member of the Universal Human Equality's
local sub-branch
with or without emotional turn-on.

Half price for under-sixteen-year-olds and soldiers.

EXCAVATION

Others dig for gold
or drill the earth
for oil,

I probe my soul.

Beneath my rank, clothes and skin
I'm already at my heart,
which, like a volcano,
can erupt any moment
and yet, one day—will be extinct.

In unknown regions
I excavate further and further.
My diamond-tipped drill, self-awareness,
is already knocking at the border
of being and annihilation,

yet even now I only know
what I always knew:
that I know absolutely nothing.

I've reached an impenetrable layer,
and the wind flapping
the nappies of newborns
on the clothes line
is like a strange signal

that life

already at the cradle
surrenders itself

to death.

THE KNIGHT OF RHYME

On a moonlit autumn evening
the Knight of Rhyme dropped in.
He cast a spell on my poem
with his sacred incantations,
and all my passion disappeared.

The poor thing was hatless,
his necktie was frayed.
I told him he could stay,
I'll give him shelter,
patch up his clothes.

He looked me straight in the eye—
mighty was the inspiration,
all the bells were ringing, chiming,
binging, bonging, clanging, gonging.

Whistling the tune of a poem by Heine,
still fixing me with his soulful eyes,
"Son," he said, "you're no heretic

there are saints without rhymes."

HIS HAIR WAS PROBABLY BLOND

and his mother called him Little Sun,
the Sun of her life
that rose radiantly
when the boy first looked at her
with two big eyes.

       Now he lies here in the museum
       under a glass top, his scalp blackened
       and the guide rapidly (other groups are waiting),
       explains that the child's body
       is 2,500 years old.

"So he's a mummy," asks in a precise voice
the bespectacled Reich German,
"yes," replies the guide, and the group
rushes on.

A young woman lingers, she looks around
hesitantly, then steps up close to the glass
and fixes her gaze on the child.

       "Little Sun," she says,
       "the Sun of my life
       went down
       when you last looked at me
       with your big eyes,"

and she can't continue
because a new group is coming,
and they might think that she's crazed.

She moves away,
and the child who had been dead for 2,500 years
stays under the glass top.

"So he's a mummy," asks in a precise voice
another Reich German,
"yes," replies the guide, and the group
rushes on.

The hall has been emptied,
but in the air
like some fine perfume, wafts

a 2,500-year-old anguish.

MATHEMATICS

The concluding formula of my life:
two unknowns over—nothing.

Two antipodes: the world and I,
at long last, successfully brought together
on a common denominator.

Until now every current ran through us
as in a Leyden jar—
the world conducted itself far from me,
and I, too, stood outside of it.

But then I became wiser,
since the purpose of my life is—nothing,
why wouldn't we make out together
when the meaning of the world is none other?

Until now I was an individual,
now I'm a collective person,

and across the green table
I confer about the "BIG NOTHING"
with the world.

MEMBERS OF THE PARTY

At the onset, the party had five members.
It's slogan was: victory or death!

Of the five, one was the president,
another the vice president,
the third was the secretary,
the fourth the treasurer,
and the fifth the manager.
And all of them going for the final victory.

Later, the party had six members,
but none of them paid a membership fee,
preferring to draw a salary.
And they conferred about it all.

Later still (because victory was running late),
the president resigned, and the vice president,
secretary, treasurer and manager,
one after the other hurried to follow him.

Since instead of victory
death became their fate,
the poet is in a quandary—
What can I do?
Tomorrow I'll cancel the old daily
and subscribe to the new.

If to such a tried-and-true party member
even this is of no help—well then,
I'll get a calling card made,
and with the neatest letters
I'll write on it nicely
that you can kiss my ass.

AT 7.20 P.M. THE ORIENT EXPRESS ROLLED IN

At 7.20 pm the Orient Express rolled in, counting from the left, on the second set of tracks.

Its snorting locomotive bore itself into the vapory lights under the glass roof, and the stoker, worn out by his hard work, wiped the perspiration off his brow and uttered a sigh of relief.

His shift was over and he looked happily towards the waiting room where his kerchiefed wife and their two children were waiting for him.

The row of carriages gave a last sensuous quiver in memory of the exhilarating weightlessness of speed, and the impatient passengers nervously tossed their bags through the windows of the sleeping compartments.

Porters rushed, baggage cars clanked, and kisses and shouts of joy trumpeted life's far-ringing sounds into the heart of the night.

Life and today surged and bubbled out of nine carriages; but at the end of the train, in a sealed wagon, lay yesterday's son: a dead man.

They brought him back from Paris, where he had suffered a heart attack, and in spite of the fact that he had dictated the pace on nine stock exchanges, he now lay rigidly in his metal coffin which was equipped with a glass lid.

Through the thick glass, his fixed eyes stared at the Moon's optically distorted face, and this is how he talked to himself in the coffin:

> "I came home because the hands of the clock stopped on the dial of my life, and Time, the watch-maker of infinite time, said 'enough—no further!' I acquiesce, let it be as my doctor told me one year ago, when he said that with my present lifestyle I would not survive past a year. Let medicine have its due, because by now I want to give everyone their due; but regretfully I could not heed the warning because in Minneapolis the price of grain fell 2 points, in London a new Steel Trust was formed, and in Berlin I had to buy graphite.
>
> Life carried me in her lap, and I sucked exciting torments from her breast; and now, here I am, staring rigidly at what our eternal travelling companion, the Moon, is doing."

Thus he mumbled to himself on the train that had carried him from Paris to Bucharest with living, loving, suffering, swaying people, who never considered that at the back of every train crouches: helplessness.

At 7.30 pm the train driver gave his report to the station master, who, having received the delivery slip for one, that is to say, one dead man, returned to his office.

I'M A KNOT IN THE PLANK OF SOCIETY

and they'll never make
a comfortable armchair out of me
for the top ten thousand

because life's lathe
doesn't work on me.

I realize that this is ingratitude
towards the Wood monopoly,
which, from the cradle to the coffin
delivers everything
door to door,
a most obliging service,
for the appropriate profit.

But it is easier to be a splinter in the timber
than a polished slab in my own eyes.

Because wood and sawdust you can get
wholesale or retail,
but for polished, glossy good manners
you have to peel off
your convictions and your individuality.

So go, lead a happy life,
become a desk
upon which they write declarations of war,
a bed to enjoy a cheap embrace on,

but consider

that the time may come
when they'll make
everything out of steel,

and then
the Wood monopoly will also
become bankrupt.

ANSWER TO THE AGITATOR!

Why should I gnash my teeth
when it won't frighten anyone?

My illusions have already worn out—

why should my teeth
wear out as well?

Does it matter
if with a single gesture
I get rid of
ten million whys?

If I were to ask them
 one by one,

I still wouldn't get an answer
to any one of them.

Does anything make a difference?

The word remains just a word,
and if they don't like it
they squeeze the daylight out of you—

and the corpse of a right winger
is just as violaceous
as the most savage left winger's.

Is there an idea here, a goal or understanding?

One should eat, drink,
have a good time,
and if it's done
a bit cleverly,

one can even avoid

procreation.

IT'S NOT AS IF I WANTED TO BRAG

It's not as if I wanted to brag,

the woman
I spent last night with
today sent a message
with an acquaintance:

she has succeeded in dry-cleaning
this dark stain
from her memory.

After that, believe me,

I haven't the least intention
of seducing the Venus de Milo
and am happy to seek
my Muse's
paternal affiliation—

I'll take extra lessons from him
about manliness.

After all, poetry is a private matter!

THE SCHOOL CHILDREN

There's no schoolbag on their backs
nor lunch box hanging by their side
and yet, hand in hand
(all of them have a perfect mark for conduct)
only on the policeman's signal
do they go from
    left
         to right.

The bib hanging on their necks says:
        "Editor's favourite,"
and if they catch sight of the Master—
they greet him in sing-song unison
while inwardly they'll add:
thank you for the instructions.

As a rule they marry young,
so that they can be considered 'grown-up poets'.

They derive their ideals from the older generation,
and the only reason they don't reverentially
fall on their belly in front of them is
because they're so slender—

they don't have a belly.

In the hope of recognition
they sit in the coffee house all day long
trying to get to know
more and more people.

And they produce so-called 'ready-made' products
which, in accordance with the buyer's wishes,
they're happy to alter at any time.
Incidentally, for all they care, you could die, no worries,
because they're only interested in immortality
and anyway, why should they be rebellious?

They recognize that Shakespeare was a great poet,
and they endeavour to be decent craftsmen.

If the truth be known, none of them is a poet,
just a very limited liability
literary shareholding company
for the purpose of producing mass-versification.

And they all push and shove so hard
that instead of their hands they'll need

their elbows manicured.

THE LITANY OF VAINLINESS

In vain do you give them
the Legion of Honor, the Iron Cross
or commemorative badges of war—
instead of their legs
you can only give them wooden legs,
and instead of their eyes
only glass eyes.

In vain do you give them
graves of honor in the cemetery,
and in vain you give war pensions
to their widows—
you cannot give back their lives,
and if they were alive, they would refuse
your farthings.

In vain you sent them
into the firing line:
before the assault
the shopkeeper was thinking
how much today's takings
must have been back home,
and the peasant
that around this time the harvesters
are returning from the wheat fields—
and now I roar at you
the accusation:
it was not soldiers you sent
to the front,
but humans beings.

In vain you killed them
and in vain will you kill us,
who write poems
against war,
and it is precisely this that is maddening,
that all of us are afraid
and dreading it,
yet every word and
every struggle is in vain:
one of these days
we will still be mobilized.

FOR A HUMAN I'M TOO MUCH OF A POET

For a human I'm too much a poet,
and for a poet
I'm excessively human.

Words like 'ivy'
envelop my body
and conceal
my flaky plaster.

Those who look at me from afar
believe in me,
but intimates know
that I, too, am just
made of mortar.

My body is an abandoned castle,
and my soul—
this poor home-bound soul
can't reach home.

Among people
I like solitude,
and from solitude
I escape to the crowd
to be alone.

IT HAPPENED AT NOON TODAY

As I was walking down the street
two unruly, cheeky rays of sunshine
laughed so impertinently behind me

that in my embarrassment
the middle of my back turned sweaty.

"Hey there," hailed a distant voice,
"the violets have long been naked,
aren't you ashamed of yourself,
still in an overcoat?"

Perhaps you think
there was more to it?
No, no.
That was it.

Then I stepped up close to a dilapidated
bench on the boulevard,
patted it chummily on the shoulder
and whispered in its ear

"So what do you reckon, old boy?
Spring is here!"

THE FORTUNE TELLER

It was love at first sight!
Then and there,
before even knowing her name,
pale as the moon and stuttering,
Maurice asked her to marry him.

*

Jeanette and Maurice were wed.
They loved each other ... lah-di-dah.
"Tomorrow we'll go see a fortune teller,"
said Maurice, arriving home one evening.
"Let's find out what the future holds,
how long our happiness will last."

*

Having received 10 francs per person,
the following day
the fortune teller told them:

"You will live together in happiness
and ever-lasting love ."
"And how many children will we have?"
asked Jeanette solemnly.
"In your palm I see five, Madame,
and in yours, Monsieur—
the lines show two."

WHEN GOD CREATED

When God created
the Managing Director
and the typist,
he said to them:

Go and multiply,
like the Mills & Boon romances,
so that there may finally be
happy endings on earth.

But they didn't listen to the Lord,
started worshipping a new god
called 'Gynaecologist',

who, being a gentleman of certain social standing,
a very quiet and tactful god,
didn't ask
who the father was—
he, citing medical confidentiality,
nullified what the Other One wisely created.

SELF-IMPOSED EXILE

I don't go to the movies or to the theater,
and I am not a subscriber to Radio.

I do not read the editorials,
and to the ammunition manufacturers'
public meetings
I return their invitations.

I don't give to the beggars
from my unemployment benefit,
and I am no longer bothered by:

the luxuriously-kept mistresses of others.

Hitler and the latest from the Telegraphic News Service
do not interest me,
    what would interest me—
    cannot interest me.

So, long live the decent persons'
last refuge:

    self-imposed exile.

NEITHER EXECUTIONER NOR MARTYR

Preaching water,
why shouldn't you drink wine?

After all, conviction
is not a cloak-room ticket,
whereby one is compelled
to redeem one's own principles.

Take me for instance:

I want to be neither
executioner nor martyr,

to be responsible
for killing or dying in another's name—
and for me there's no law

other than my own—

and the reason I won't kill
is not because the law forbids it,

I will not kill
even when the law permits it.

I am free,

infinitely freer
than one who is bound hand and foot
by his professed credo

because I never
sublet my soul

to another's belief.

TO ADHERE AIRTIGHT

I'd like to be your brief Lycra swim suit
so that I could adhere airtight to your naked body.

I'd like to be your long-lasting lipstick
so that I could survive the kisses of other men.

I'd like to be your migraine
so that for once I could also torment you,

and I'd like to be Bayer's aspirin
to relieve your pain.

LIKE A CURSED EX-CROWN PRINCE

Like a cursed ex-crown prince,
who's now a used-car salesman,

I can never be so reborn
that I wouldn't cause pain
to my mother.

I can never so shave
that my beard wouldn't regrow,
and with the passage of years,
my skin having become too tight for me,
I look back, and tomorrow
is behind me.

And like cattle that stares at the new gate
which is so reminiscent of the old one,
that's how I look in the mirror,

and step by step proceed
towards the slaughter.

COMING TO TERMS WITH THE IMPOSSIBLE

From this day onward
I will not make copies of my letters,
nor will I maintain a double entry
of my good and bad deeds,

and if my fate so requires, the 140,000 heartbeats
together with 28,000 deep breaths
which I've received from life on a daily loan thus far
I will assign to death.

Oh, because I am such a long-standing debtor
of everyone here on earth,
as illustrated by the circumstances under which
I came into this world:

already in my childhood I received a legal writ,
the content of which was the

TEN COMMANDMENTS

and the old Scripture teacher emphatically warned me
that I must absolutely honor the contract
I entered into upon my birth
with the Lord of Heaven,
otherwise I would go to hell.

Since then, I've even signed promissory notes,

shouldered the rules of Civil, Commercial,
Domestic, Criminal and Constitutional Law,
and tried, at all times, to fulfill

my obligations under International Law—
furthermore, I entered into newer and newer agreements
with various (Minister-of-the-Interior-approved)
    organisations.

So, little by little, my life became filled with more and
    more

permission, command, law and rule.
I didn't smoke on the tram, although I would have liked to
and I never fished in forbidden season

and though I staggered under the weight of the burdens,
I always abided by regulations
because I knew what were

decency and responsibility.

I was born naked and free,
and I let them put me into clothes,
and in accordance with social customs
I did not remove my little coat in company
even when I felt too hot

because I tried to tie myself to the community
with more and more strings.
And behold, now they still want to bankrupt me
because according to the demands of racial purity
I can't officially prove

that I am actually descended from Adam.

My God, don't be surprised then
that I cracked under the weight of the burdens,

since they seized my belief in civilization
and perhaps by tomorrow they will auction it—

and after all this, all I ask of You
is to allow me to reach a forced settlement
for the only remaining things of importance
to me in life:

    the clouds, the flowers, my mother
    and the one who loves me,
      for that short duration, while life still lasts.

Lord! I've tried to live honorably,
and now, given these few percent,

    I—most respectfully—

come to terms with the impossible.

HEADS OR TAILS

Heads or tails—muttered the suicide-to-be
and took out his last coin.
If it's heads—I'll have dinner for the last time and throw
myself in the Danube—
if it's tails—I'll buy some rope and hang myself.
The coin flew up in the air, and the suicide-to-be tried to
explain his bizarre decision to himself.

If it's heads—I'll throw myself in the Danube because
    there is mindlessness on earth,
so fate had lied.
In one country anarchy rages, in another people line up
to offer their last drop of blood under the slogans of
    nationalism.
In one country, gold in its boredom
travels underground,
in another, every year 2 million people die of starvation.
Some nations are members of the League of Nations and
are arming themselves,
other nations are not members and are waging war.

Humanity is evil and is sentenced to death!

Unable to understand the concept of love across the
    millennia, what is the human head
good for other than chewing?
If it's heads—I'll have dinner and throw myself in the
    Danube.

The coin reached the highest point of its ascent and
    started to fall.

If it's tails, I'll hang myself, because what does it say?
The writing says: don't steal, don't cheat, don't kill!
and people steal, cheat and kill.
(Here for a moment his thoughts came to a standstill.)
What if the writing said: steal, cheat, kill!
It became clear to him that in loving coexistence,
humanity would have long ago degenerated—because it's exactly
those deeds and thoughts that advanced human civilization
... which sanctified stealing, cheating and killing!

If it's tails—I'll hang myself because the writing was mendacious.

Heads or tails—muttered the suicide-to-be, and his last coin fell into the drain.

He didn't hang himself because he didn't have the money for rope and,
not budging from his decision, he didn't throw himself in the Danube
because he couldn't have dinner for the last time.

So the poor man starved to death, like every person who has principles and sticks to them.

BECOME A MESSAGE

Become a message
        to the East, the West,
            the North and the South,
every which way
where people are living.

Be a tiny light in the terrible night,
a guiding beacon—
and signal that there are still those for whom
a song is a song
and music is music.

There are ones who, bending over a microscope,
research unexplained death,
who are not interested in today or tomorrow
        but the day after tomorrow!

There are still people for whom
the cost of a painting's varnish matters not,
for whom believing
is not about business
or credit!

And there are lights everywhere,
though now just solitary, orphan flames—
but one day they may all turn into a cleansing fire
        that could redeem
        the world!

Become a whispered message
            to every place on earth
            and to every region of the sky
that apart from thieves and murderers

there are also human beings.

TRANSLATOR'S AFTERWORD

Lajos Walder (1913-1945), poet, playwright and lawyer, was my father.

I have no personal recollections of him. Though in my childhood, we had a large photo of him on the wall in our apartment. We knew that he was a poet, who wrote under the pseudonym 'Vándor'.

*

In 1987, two years before to the fall of communism in Hungary, my father was commemorated in an hour-long tribute on Radio Budapest—"Remembering the Memorable Lajos Vándor."

"It all began in 1932," Géza Hegedüs, the venerable doyen of Hungarian letters, reminisced on the program. "One afternoon, the door of the editorial office of Anonymous Publishers was opened by a round-faced young man who was, by the standards of the time, dressed in a bodgie fashion. His manner was provocatively arrogant. He wasn't tall, but he was all muscle, and under his slick black hair his face was smiling. I well recall him saying the following, word for word:

> 'My name is Lajos Vándor, I am a poet, a law student and a trainee worker at the knitting mills. To the proletarians I am a rotten bourgeois; to the bourgeoisie I am a stinking proletarian; to the petit-bourgeoisie I am an evil anarchist and to the anarchists I am a cowardly petit-bourgeois. And everybody is right, whatever they say about me. But I wrote a few masterpieces—which the poets and *les belles âmes* would call prose, and the prose writers and modern aesthetes would call poems. Take them

and eat them, read them and publish them; but first give me a cigarette because I left my cash register at home, and I don't have four cents in my pocket to buy a single fag.'

As I was reading his poems, I was gripped with the feeling that I had rarely sensed such a completely accurate expression of our times. This was fright, anxiety and profound indignation mixed with bizarre humor."

*

My father was then just nineteen years old. One of the poems he handed to the young men in the editorial office was "I am a Wanderer," in which he creates his poetic identity and establishes the reason for his choice of the pseudonym 'Vándor'—meaning 'wanderer'. "We, the Twenty-Five Letters of the Alphabet" was another poem he showed them at this time. (The letters number twenty-five, by the way, because 'W' is missing from the Hungarian alphabet; its use is restricted to German names and words).

The following year, the Budapest publisher Anonymous brought out *Heads or Tails*, my father's first collection of poetry. His second collection, *Group Portrait*, appeared in Budapest in 1938, from Cserépfalvi Publishers . There would be no further publications during my father's lifetime: after 1938, works by Jews could no longer be published in Hungary.

*

Géza Hegedüs' 1987 assessment of my father's work included the following remarks:

> What a sensation it was for us to hear that particular voice. His outstandingly recitable and highly effective free verse was well known during the 1930s be-

cause the most popular presenters of the time were keen to recite it. His uniquely-voiced poetry was written with enormous compositional care. He carefully planned what appeared to be careless, and polished it until it was exactly as careless as he intended it to be. He lived not quite thirty-two years. He had two volumes of poetry published. Their content is fifty poems, with not a single inferior one among them.

Once, with his usual self-sarcasm, he said to me: "I only write my selected works." In an era of entirely pessimistic hopelessness, he heralded gentle humanity and tried to find some measure of comfort in the joy of knowing how to laugh. It is with this laughter, this manly humor, that he rose above his own despair ...

But who remembers him today? Our literary history doesn't mention his name, and even the *Lexicon of Literature* devotes only a few lines to him, informing us that Lajos Vándor (1913-1945) was a poet, that fascism took him away, and that since then all trace of him had disappeared ...

I feel it is my job to let the reading public know that there was a poet called Lajos Vándor, who was the most credible voice to express the times between the two world wars. Without this artist's entirely individualistic voice, the overall picture of that period is incomplete.

*

My father was born in Budapest in June 1913. Both of his parents were Jewish. He was the first child of his mother and the fourth child of his father, who had been widowed earlier and left with three small children—my father's two sisters and older brother. The latter were raised

Catholic in accordance with their mother's faith. My father's younger brother, Imre, was born two and a half years after him.

My grandfather, who served in the Austro-Hungarian army throughout World War I ('Jews now had the opportunity to prove their patriotism'), was forcibly retired without a pension during an upsurge of anti-semitism in 1919. He died early, when my father was only eleven years old. My grandmother, in spite of enormous hardships, was determined to raise all the children together. For many years, they led a hand-to-mouth existence. Light and gas were never left on a moment longer than necessary (—with that in mind, my father refers to himself as "an economy stove's blazing flame" in "Group Portrait of Myself"). But they were a close-knit family, where everyone fasted on the Jewish Day of Atonement, while also celebrating Christmas.

By the time my father obtained his baccalaureate, the *numerus clausus* severely restricted Jewish students' access to university. Because he passed his examinations with straight distinctions, he was one of a handful of Jews allowed to enroll, and graduated with a J.D. in 1937. In the meantime, he wrote poetry, published and edited the highly respected literary monthly *Cross Section*, which appeared on the newsstands for the then record time of two years. He worked as a factory hand to earn a living, and also as a children's program presenter on the radio, for which he wrote fairy tales. In addition, always in the hope of making a living by his writing, he composed and published short stories. But he saw himself first and foremost as a poet.

*

The 1930s were an increasingly difficult time in Hungary, which was still chafing under the aftermath of World

War I and, like other nations, suffering the fallout from the Stock Market Crash of 1929. Following the Treaty of Trianon in 1920, flags in Hungary were lowered to half-mast for eighteen years, until—infamously—it began profiting from its alliance with the Axis powers.

The country was under authoritarian, aristocratic and repressive rule. Thus, "Mr. Somogyi," the eponymous protagonist of my father's "Everyday Ode," was "once, for three weeks, /... held in jail under investigation." The Communist party was banned (after being briefly in power in 1919); yet, as noted in "Delicate Question," my father spotted "salaried communist agitators" on the streets of Budapest.

*

By the mid-1930s, beggars lined the streets and university-trained engineers were happy to be hired as tram conductors. Since jobs were scarce, employees were treated harshly. At the same time, a mundane clerical position with the government was still considered unshakeable security, as pointedly captured in the image of "the government-pensioned village bull" in "Animal Tale."

Censorship was extremely stringent—in "100% Poem," my father rates it at around forty-five percent. Radical nationalist and fascist politicians were clamoring for "solving the Jewish Question." Hungary was increasingly aligning itself with Nazi Germany. Irredentism and talk of racial purity became all-pervasive. There was a general scramble toward trying to prove one's ancestry. The putative discovery of some ancient Hungarian lineage was commonplace by necessity. Ordinary people suddenly 'learned' that there were prefixes to their family names—an instant link to the aristocracy. Which must have prompted my father to observe, in "Short Lyrical

Oration," that "everybody / is his own publicity chief, / printing error / and female cousin."

Mussolini was not only highly respected in Hungagary's official circles, but he was also popular with the man in the street. The specter of war loomed large by the mid-1930s, when the Duce's Abyssinian campaign triggered a major conflict with England, as thematized in "Telephone."

The threat of tuberculosis (and venereal disease, syphilis above all) was ubiquitous—which is palpably, if obliquely, reflected in the sociopolitical "fever" that turns into "constant temperature" in "I Was About Fifteen Years Old."

Religion flourished. People imagined themselves 'irreproachably good' if they were Christian and traditional. "God, country, family" went the slogan. The public was fed on patriotic verbiage—"it's sweet and glorious to die for the homeland"—and was also taken in by such 'perfect citizens' as the editor in "Topic for an Editorial," that "role model for the middle class" bound to "go to Heaven by car."

Fatalism thrived. Fate, the unchangeable, had a ring of truth. Thus, the line, "fate had lied"—from "Heads or Tails"—must have felt novel and daring at the time.

Anti-semitism was rampant. The Arrow Cross Party, whose ideology was similar to Nazism, was founded in 1935. Jews were barred from almost all avenues in society. Poignantly, in "Taking a Bird's Eye View of My Life," my father notes: "my grey eye / constantly shows: / *Verboten!*" And later, in "Coming to Terms With the Impossible," he observes that in spite of all his efforts to tie himself to the community, it still wished to bankrupt him "because according to the demands of racial purity / I can't officially prove // that I'm actually descended from Adam." It was in the midst of these circumstances that my father declared, in "First Person Singular": "I renounce that stupid herd, / which entrusts itself to the instincts of others."

Always an iconoclast, he wanted to unmask and break down fallacies—to bring about an awareness of the need to examine the 'old', to show up its errors or downright lies, and not to continue in chronic misery just because it had been good enough for the last few hundred years. After every disappointment he was always communicating the jolting findings, in a desperate hope to enlighten. In an era of sanctimonious determinism, he affirmed that the only 'way out' was via the evolution of the individual.

He was an early feminist. A topic to which he often returned, for instance in "Key Poem," was men's inadequate understanding and treatment of women. Generally speaking, he regarded women as emotionally more advanced than men, but considered androgyny, as he avers in "Arm in Arm," a natural and indispensable part of his own manhood.

In the 1930s, giving birth to an illegitimate child was viewed as utterly shameful, the greatest disgrace. My father's sarcastic and humorous take on this is salient in "Ode to a Free Verse."

He was a voracious reader not only of literature. Although his desire to travel was never realized (with the exception of short trips to Vienna and my parents' honeymoon in Yugoslavia), he had a keen curiosity about the world. Consequently, even though he didn't speak English, the dog's eyes in "Mooky" say "Hello, boy" in English, and "Miss Mabel Faithful" is an appropriate name for an Anglo-American tabloid reporter in "Report."

*

By the time my father obtained his law degree in 1937, no law firm in Budapest would hire a Jew, and in 1938 the first Jewish Law barred Jews from practicing in the professions. Thus, my father was only able to get a job as a laborer in a stocking factory. It was then that he had a calling card made with the following writing on it:

Dr. Lajos Vándor
Factory-Hand and Lyrical Poet

*

My parents married in 1939. My mother, Eva Lustig, is the "you" in "Parliamentarianism" and "Art Gallery." It was to her that my father wrote "Expedition", and was later to write "Moments" and "Music for Prose."

In 1940, my parents' first child, my brother Peter, was born. In the same year forced labor went into effect in Hungary. Jewish males, forbidden to join the Hungarian army, were to serve in forced labor battalions. Avoidance was tantamount to treason. In 1941, Hungary entered the war as an ally of Nazi Germany. Through the early part of 1942, my father and his younger brother, Imre, served in the same forced labor battalion. By May of that year, the battalion turned out to have too many men, and because my father was already a family man, he was transferred to another battalion in the vicinity of Budapest.

For a while, there were periods of furlough, and he was able to live at home. By that stage, holding down even a factory job between call-ups was out of the question. It was during that period that he must have written his three plays: "Vase of Pompeii", "Tyrtaeus" and "Below Zero".

*

The Germans occupied Hungary on March 19, 1944. Systematic deportation of the Jewish population (starting with the provinces) began immediately. In early November 1944, when the Russians had already reached the outskirts of Budapest, all locally-stationed forced labor battalions were herded towards Austria on death marches. My father reached Mauthausen. During the final few weeks of the war, he was interned in Gunskirchen.

U.S. troops liberated Gunskirchen on May 4, 1945. My father, along with other survivors, including Géza Hegedüs, walked through the opened gates and accepted a can of meat from an American soldier. They had had almost nothing to eat for weeks. He must also have been suffering from Typhus. Almost immediately after he ate, he developed terrible stomach cramps, and died a few hours later, on a straw mattress in a makeshift hospital.

*

My father's mother, my mother—pregnant with my sister—my brother Peter and my eighteen-month-old self were liberated from the ghetto by the Russians. My father was never to see his third child, Nina ('Ninotchka'), born a month later. Her birth was aided by a Jewish captain in the Red Army. Mercifully, at that time, the family had not yet received news of my father's death.

*

In the difficult postwar years in Budapest, my late mother tried repeatedly to have my father's work republished, or have his plays performed. Most of these efforts were heartbreakingly unsuccessful because in Hungary, from the early 1950s onward, no literature was considered relevant unless it had communist themes. My father's work, with its profoundly humanistic bent and strong focus on the individual, did not meet those requirements. Even less so since he had an equal contempt for both fascism and communism, as poignantly articulated in "Last Human Being."

*

After the war, my mother, Eva, married Alexander Endrey, who was the most wonderful second father to the three of us. My younger sister, Linda, was born to this marriage.

During the 1956 uprising, one very cold and frightening November night, our family, in just the clothes we were wearing and one haversack for the greatest essentials between us, walked across no man's land into Austria. Some months later, we arrived in Sydney, Australia.

In 1961, my grandmother, Ida Walder, was able to follow us. The things she could bring with her were severely restricted and closely scrutinized. However, no one suspected that the bundles of age-old, yellowed and torn manuscripts she had packed in her trunk were anything other than the sentimental memorabilia of an old lady. That is how my father's unpublished manuscripts reached Sydney!

*

The unspoken responsibility of one day achieving publication of my father's works in Hungary was left to us, his children.

For years, I had been sorting and organizing my father's prolific output of unpublished works. I did this slowly; often needing to stop for a while because it was too painful. By 1987, the manuscripts were in good order. Then the inconceivable happened. Censorship in Hungary relaxed in the wake of *glasnost*, and the door of possibility opened: two years later, after counltess phone calls and extensive correspondence from the other side of the world, the posthumous volume of my father's selected poems—*A Poet Lived Here Amongst You* (*Egy költő élt itt közöttetek*)—was published in Hungary.

When the book came out in September, 1989, I was in Budapest with my uncle, the late Imre Walder. We appeared on Hungarian television together with Géza Hegedüs and an actor who recited "Budapest Division," "Mr. Somogyi, or the Everyday Ode" and "Music for Prose." In the post-communist mood of the time, my father's poem "Interview" was chosen as the October poem of the month on the Poetry Program of Budapest Television. Almost a year later, two of my father's three plays, "Vase of Pompeii" and "Tyrtaeus," were published in a volume entitled *Pompeji*. In 1991, I began translating my father's work.

*

Géza Hegedüs was not the only Hungarian critic to claim that my father's work differed from traditional Hungarian poetry. Thus, Gábor Thurzó, a well-known novelist and dramaturge wrote:

> Lajos Vándor has neither ancestor nor partner in Hungarian literature. He is a poet, without a doubt a lyricist through and through, yet one whose every line and every poetic breath is pure heresy, pure rebellion against accustomed forms of poetry.

The truth of this assessment provided personal cause for rejoicing because it contained the essence of my opportunity to successfully render his works in English. Hungarian is a very different language from English—it is far more 'long-winded'. And yet, I continued to marvel at the economy and brevity of my father's expressions, written seven or eight decades ago.

He was contemptuous of the many who still wrote 'pretty' poetry, as he notes in "Obligatory Spring Poem."

In "The School Children," he calls such versifiers "a very limited liability / literary share holding company / for the purpose of producing mass-versification." His break with the most esteemed poetic tradition was deliberate. He wanted to use everyday language in poetry. Yet, behind his ordinary speaking voice, there is always a deeper philosophical content.

He was not a fan of Surrealist poetry, and he parodies it in "Autobiography," for example. He did not think that it offered great challenges of style. On a philosophical level, he disapproved of the Surrealist movement's alignment with Marxist orthodoxy. He did not believe that literature should be associated with any political party. Unlike his Surrealist contemporaries, he would not abandon reason in light of the horrors perpetrated in World War I. Instead, in his numerous anti-war poems he reminds the reader of the deaths, glass eyes, wooden legs and grieving caused by that war. And while the bulk of the population ostensibly continued in ignorant hypocrisy, he did not want "to be responsible / for killing or dying in another's name," as he proclaims in "Neither Executioner Nor Martyr."

*

"The opus that stunned me the most was his poem 'Members of the Party' because it's as if its stanzas follow virtually point for point the histories of the parties which came into being after the change of regime," wrote journalist András Nyerges in the Budapest literary magazine *Kritika* in 2005. In particular, Nyerges was commenting on the remarkable clarity of the poet, whose descriptions in the 1930s proved particularly accurate to the chaotic emergence of political parties following the collapse of communism in 1989.

*

My father's most abiding concern as a man and a poet was for the individual and individual conscience. In one of his notebooks, I found the following notation:

> but what am I to do,
> I am not willing to turn myself inside out
> and will journey on with the soul
> even if
> around me everyone has already buttoned their
> conscience
> up to the chin.

And so, in "Traveling," on a shaky wooden bench, "the soul travels on" with him.

*

My brother Peter, with his criticism and editing, my sisters Nina and Linda in all other ways, have been with me every step of this journey. Our children and grandchildren, who do not speak Hungarian, are now able to read my father's work!

It has been my family's decision that the English translations of my father's poetry and plays should appear under his family name 'Walder', so as to ensure that the connection to his descendants remain clear.

*

The original manuscripts of his unpublished works are now in the Archives of Yad Vashem, Jerusalem.

*

In 2004, Macmillan Australia, published *We, the Twenty-Five Letters of the Alphabet: English Translations from the Selected Poems of the late Lajos Walder*. This volume contained forty-four poems (it was all I had ready in English at the time). In 2007, Macmillan Australia also published *The*

Dramas of Lajos Walder, containing "Vase of Pompeii," "Tyrtaeus," and "Below Zero." I remain grateful to Jenny Zimmer, at the time Art Publisher of Macmillan Australia, for her steadfast support of the work.

In 2012, I had the good fortune of contacting Dr. Michael Eskin of Upper West Side Philosophers, Inc.

Agnes Walder

NOTES

p. 19   *"Tour Guide as Foreword"*: "Gather Around Yourself" is the introductory poem to *Group Portrait* (1938), the second and last collection of poems Lajos Walder published during his lifetime.

p. 21   "a publisher in Academia": in the early 1930s in Hungary, the notion of a publisher in academia was unthinkable.

p. 28   "pengő" (from the onomatopoetic "peng", which captures the ringing sound of coins): the Hungarian currency between 1927-1946.

p. 48   "Petőfi": Sándor Petőfi (1823-1849) is considered Hungary's national poet; a key figure in the revolution of 1848, he died in battle at the age of twenty-six.

"mattress-grave": toward the end of his life, the poet Heinrich Heine (1797-1856) famously referred to himself as living in a "mattress-grave."

p. 75   "just Louis": the poet's given name "Lajos" is equivalent to the French "Louis."

p. 91   "purulent Europe": this poem was composed in an era when even the most progressive liberals considered Europe the pinnacle of culture and civilization; thus, Hungarian left-wing poet Attila József wrote a famous poem in honor of Thomas Mann's visit to Budapest in 1937, entitled "Greetings for Thomas Mann," which concludes by saying: while most of the assembled will listen to Thomas Mann's story-telling, there will be those who will merely gaze at him for the joy of "seeing here, today, / among whites, a European."

p. 106   "Ancient or New Alliance": according to Hungarian oral tradition, Árpád (son of Álmos) was the leader who unified the Magyar tribes through a covenant of blood—the poem's "Ancient" alliance; "New Alliance" refers to Hungary's siding with Nazi Germany.

p. 131   "parish cemetery of Downe": upon Darwin's death, his family arranged for him to be buried in St Mary's Churchyard in Downe; however, at the behest of William Spottiswode, the president of the Royal Society, the Dean of Westminster agreed for Darwin to be buried at Westminster Abbey—a fact the poet was apparently unaware of.

p. 144   "modify Napoleon's words": Napoleon is reported as saying, "Every French soldier carries a French marshal's baton in his knapsack [Tout soldat français porte dans sa giberne le bâton de marèchal de France]."

ACKNOWLEDGMENTS

With my love and thanks to the memory of my late husband, Dr. Bernie Silberstein, for his unfailing support. He was my first reader in English. While he couldn't help with the actual translation—he did not speak Hungarian —his wonderful command of English was a treasure chest for me.

My late uncle, Imre Walder, and my father were close brothers. My uncle's recall of personal and historical matters, and the breadth of his literary knowledge of their times were invaluable. I am grateful for our loving collaboration which lasted over two decades.

*

Always with my love and thanks: to my brother, Dr. Peter Endrey-Walder, and my sisters, Nina Sekel and Linda Kopcho. It would have been inconceivable for me to achieve either the Hungarian posthumous publications or the English translations without them.

To my sons, Drs. Paul and Robbie Silberstein, for their love, profound understanding, and for reminding me that I am realizing my dreams.

To my nieces and nephews—in particular, to Kim Haimovic and Ronny Endrey-Walder for their help.

To our treasured grandchildren, who will one day be cognizant of their great-grandfather's work.

* * *

Some of the poems here gathered were originally published in *Heads or Tails* (*Fej vagy irás*; Budapest: Anonymous, 1933) and *Group Portrait* (*Csoportkép*; Budapest: Cserépfalvi, 1938). A good number were republished posthumously in *A Poet Lived Here Amongst You* (*Egy költő él itt közöttetek*; Budapest: Maecenas, 1989), which also contained previously unpublished texts. Some of the poems have also previously appeared in English in *We, the Twenty-Five Letters of the Alphabet* (Melbourne: Macmillan 2004), and some appear in print for the first time in any language:

GATHER AROUND YOURSELF *Tour Guide as Foreword* (Csoportosulj—Önmagad Köré *Elöszó Helyett Utikalauz*, 38/89); I AM A WANDERER (Vándor Vagyok, 33/89/04); RIDING ON CLOUDS (Felhőlovaglás, 33/89); WE, THE TWENTY-FIVE LETTERS OF THE ALPHABET (Mi Az Abécé Huszonöt Betüje, 33/89/04); FAMILY CHARACTERISTICS (Családi Jellegü, 33/89); INTERVIEW (Interjú, 89/04); ARM IN ARM (Karonfogva, 38/89/04); REVERENCE (Kegyelet, 89/ 04); SHORT LYRICAL ORATION (Rövid Lirai Szónoklat, 38/89/04); TELEPHONE (Telefon, 89);THE HEAD (A Fej, 38/89/04); HOROSCOPE (Horoszkóp, 38/89/ 04); ANIMAL TALE (Állatmese, 38/89/04); INFORMATION (Információ, 38/89/04); BUDAPEST (Budapest, 38/ 89/04); LEGEND IN PROSE (Legenda Prózában, 38/89/04); LAST HUMAN BEING (Utolsó Ember, 89/04); AUTOBIOGRAPHY (Életrajz, 89/04); MOOKY (Muki, 38/ 89/04); TEN COMMANDMENTS (Tízparancsolat, 33/89); ESSENTIALLY A REVISED EDITION (Lényegében Átdolgozott Kiadás, 33/89); JAZZ ANTHEM (Jazzhimnusz, 33/89); CIRCLE (Kör, 33/89); TRAVELING (Utazás, 38/89/04); DUST CLOTH (Portörlő, 38/89); GROUP PORTRAIT OF MYSELF (Csoportkép Magamról, 38/89/04); ODE TO A FREE VERSE (Vers Egy Szabad Vershez, 38/89); A POET LIVES HERE AMONGST YOU (Egy Költő Él Itt Közöttetek, 89/04); TOPIC FOR AN EDITORIAL (Vezércikktéma, 89);COMMEMORATIVE PLAQUE (Emléktábla, 89); STUDY TOUR (Tanulmányút, 38/89/04); THE HUMAN (Ember, 38/89/ 04); REPORT (Riport, 89); FIRST PERSON SINGULAR (Egyesszám Elsőszemélyben, 38/89); DELICATE QUESTION (Kényes Kérdés, 89); WORLD HISTORY (Világtörténelem, 38/89/ 04); TYPE-

WRITER (Irógép, 38/ 89/04); THE COIN (Az Érem, 33/89); THE SEEDSMAN (A Magvető, 33/89); OBLIGATORY SPRING POEM (Kötelező Tavaszi Vers, 38/89/04); BUDAPEST DIVISION (Budapesti Hadosztály, 38/89/04); IN THE LAST FEW DAYS (Az Utolsó Napokban, 89/04); OVER THE SPEED OF 100 KILOMETERS (100 Kilométeren Felüli Sebesség, 33/89); BLOOD PACT (Vérszerződés, 33/89); LOST GENERATION (Elveszett Generáció, 38/89/04); MECHANICAL PRAYER (Gépies Ima, 33/89); HAPPINESS (Boldogság, 89); POEM OF THE UNEMPLOYED (Munkanélküli Verse, 38/89/04); KEY POEM (Kulcsvers, 33/89); NOW I CONFESS (Most Már Bevallom, 1st pub.); AT THE TOMB OF THE UNKNOWN SOLDIER (Az Ismeretlen Katona Sirjánál, 89); ACCOMPLICES (Cinkosok, 1st pub.); PARLIAMENTARIANISM (Parlamentárizmus, 38/89/04); EXPEDITION (Expedició, 89/04); AND IF IT SADDENS YOU (És Ha Elszomorit Néha Téged, 89); MOMENTS (Percek, 89/04); ART GALLERY (Képtár, 38/89/04); MUSIC FOR PROSE (Zene Prozára, 89/04); FAMILY EVENT (Családi Esemény, 38/89/04); PHILOSOPHICALLY PROFOUND POEM (Filozófiai Mélységü Költemény, 33/89/04); MEMORIAL SPEECH (Emlékbeszéd, 89/04); MR. SOMOGYI, OR THE EVERYDAY ODE (Somogyi Úr, Avagy Egy Hétköznapi Óda, 38/89/ 04); I WAS ABOUT FIFTEEN YEARS OLD (Körülbelül 15 Éves Voltam, 89/04); PEACE (Béke, 38/89/04); A POET, HIS SOUL IN WHITE TIE AND TAILS (Egy Költő Lelki-frakkban, 89); 100% POEM (Százszázalékos Vers, 38/89); MANHOOD (Férfikor, 89); THE DREAM (Az Álom, 89/04); THE 10,000,001st LOVE POEM IN PROSE (10,000,001-ik Szerelmes Vers Prózában, 33/89); ORPHAN POEM (Apátlan Anyátlan Árva Vers, 89); TAKING A BIRD'S EYE VIEW OF MY LIFE (Madártávlatból Nézem Az Életem, 89); I LIKE YOUNG, FIRM, ROUND BREASTS (Én A Gömbölyű Kemény Lánymelleket Szeretem, 1st pub.); THE LAST SPECTATOR (Az Utolsó Néző, 89/04); I SEN-

TENCE MY SELF-ESTEEM TO LIFELONG LIFE (Élet-
fogytiglani Életre Itélve, 89); WHOLESAILING (Nagykeres-
kedés, 33/89); STAR (Csillag, 89); I'M ONLY DISSIPATING
ENERGY (Én Csak Bomló Energia Vagyok, 89); FOR TWO
DOLLARS, COME ON IN, SWEETIE (Két Pengőért Gyere
Be Édes, 1st pub.); EXCAVATION (Ásatás, 89); THE
KNIGHT OF RHYME (Rimlovag, 1st pub.); HIS HAIR WAS
PROBABLY BLOND (Valószinüleg Szöke Haja Volt, 89);
MATHEMATICS (Matematika, 1st pub.); MEMBERS OF
THE PARTY (Párttagok, 89); AT 7.20 P.M. THE ORIENT EX-
PRESS ROLLED IN (Hét Óra Húszkor Robogott Be Az Ori-
ent Express, 89/04); I'M A KNOT IN THE PLANK OF
SOCIETY (Görcs Vagyok A Társadalom Deszkájában, 89);
ANSWER TO THE AGITATOR! (Valász—Az Agitátornak!,
89); IT'S NOT AS IF I WANTED TO BRAG (Nem Mintha
Dicsekedni Akarnék, 1st pub.); THE SCHOOL CHILDREN
(Az Iskolások, 1st pub.); THE LITANY OF VAINLINESS (A
Hiábavalóság Litániája, 89/04); FOR A HUMAN I'M TOO
MUCH OF A POET (Embernek Költő Vagyok / És Költőnek
Tulságosan Ember, 1st pub.); IT HAPPENED AT NOON
TODAY (Ma Délben Történt, 1st pub.); THE FORTUNE
TELLER (A Jósnő, 1st pub.); WHEN GOD CREATED (Ami-
kor Az Isten Megteremtette, 1st pub.); SELF-IMPOSED
EXILE (Önkéntes Száműzetés, 89/04); NEITHER EXECU-
TIONER NOR MARTYR (Se Hóhér, Se Mártir, 89); TO AD-
HERE AIRTIGHT (Hogy Légmentesen Tapadhassak, 1st
pub.); LIKE A CURSED EX-CROWN PRINCE (Mint Egy
Elátkozott Ex-Királyfi, 89); COMING TO TERMS WITH
THE IMPOSSIBLE (Kiegyezés A Lehetetlennel, 89/04);
HEADS OR TAILS (Fej Vagy Irás, 33/89); BECOME A MES-
SAGE (Legyen Belőled Üzenet, 89).

ALSO AVAILABLE FROM UWSP

November Rose: A Speech on Death by Kathrin Stengel
(2008 Independent Publisher Book Award)

November-Rose: Eine Rede über den Tod by Kathrin Stengel

Philosophical Fragments of a Contemporary Life
by Julien David

*17 Vorurteile, die wir Deutschen gegen Amerika und die
Amerikaner haben und die so nicht ganz stimmen können*
by Misha Waiman

The DNA of Prejudice: On the One and the Many
by Michael Eskin (2010 Next Generation Indie Book
Award for Social Change)

Descartes' Devil: Three Meditations by Durs Grünbein

Fatal Numbers: Why Count on Chance
by Hans Magnus Enzensberger

The Vocation of Poetry by Durs Grünbein
(2011 Independent Publisher Book Award)

The Waiting Game: An Essay on the Gift of Time
by Andrea Köhler

Mortal Diamond: Poems by Durs Grünbein

*Yoga for the Mind: A New Ethic for Thinking and Being &
Meridians of Thought* by Michael Eskin & Kathrin Stengel

The Wisdom of Parenthood: An Essay by Michael Eskin

*Health is in Your Hands: Jin Shin Jyutsu—Practicing the Art of
Self-Healing (With 51 Flash Cards for the Hands-On Practice
of Jin Shin Jyutsu)* by Waltraud Riegger-Krause

A Moment More Sublime: A Novel by Stephen Grant

High on Low: Harnessing the Power of Unhappiness
by Wilhelm Schmid

Become a Message: Poems
  by Lajos Walder

What We Gain As We Grow Older: On Gelassenheit
  by Wilhelm Schmid

Potentially Harmless: A Philosopher's Manhattan
  by Kathrin Stengel